T. S. WILLAN

The inland trade

Studies in English internal trade in the
sixteenth and seventeenth centuries

MANCHESTER UNIVERSITY PRESS

ROWMAN AND LITTLEFIELD

© T. S. Willan 1976

Published by
Manchester University Press
Oxford Road
Manchester M13 9PL

ISBN 0 7190 0638 4

First published in the United States 1976 by
Rowman and Littlefield
Totowa, New Jersey 07512

ISBN 0 87471 853 8

Typeset at the Minor Press
Printed and bound in Great Britain at The Pitman Press, Bath

CONTENTS

PREFACE

These studies contain omissions which need a word of explanation. The account of the movement of goods in confined to the Elizabethan period largely because a good deal has already been written on the movement of goods by water in the seventeenth century. Moreover it is not certain that a re-examination of the sources on road transport in that century would add very much to what is already known about that subject. A more serious omission is the absence of any general survey of the wholesale trade; instead of such a survey there are only a couple of case studies. The reason for this omission is not just idleness but the feeling that the history of wholesale trade has reached the point where it can best be furthered by such case studies.

One of the silent revolutions in historical research has been the provision of xerox copies of manuscripts. For such copies of manuscripts in their custody, I am grateful to the archivists of the House of Lords Record Office, the Lancashire Record Office, the Cheshire Record Office and the Archives Department of Manchester City Library. I wish to thank Dr N. J. Williams for kindly allowing me to use material from his unpublished thesis and the Library of Southampton University for similar permission in the case of Miss J. L. Wiggs's thesis. Finally Dr W. H. Chaloner first suggested to me that seventeenth-century trade tokens might be a source for the history of shops. I am very grateful to him for this fruitful suggestion.

T. S. W.

ABBREVIATIONS

Exch. K.R.—Exchequer Kings Remembrancer
Harrison, 'Description'— W. Harrison, 'Description of England',
    in R. Holinshed, *Chronicles of England*, London, 1807.
H.M.C.—Historical Manuscripts Commission
Lowe—*The diary of Roger Lowe of Ashton-in-Makerfield,
    1663–74*, ed. W. L. Sachse, 1938.
L.R.O.—Lancashire Record Office (Preston).
O.E.D.—Oxford English Dictionary.
*Shuttleworth accounts—The house and farm accounts of the
    Shuttleworths of Gawthorpe Hall*, ed. J. Harland, 4 vols. (con-
    tinuous pagination), Chetham Society, xxxv (1856), xli (1856),
    xliii (1857), xlvi (1858).
Stout—*The autobiography of William Stout of Lancaster,
    1665–1752*, ed. J. D. Marshall, Chetham Society, 3rd series, xiv
    (1967).
Williamson—G. C. Williamson, *Trade tokens issued in the
    seventeenth century*, 3 vols. (continuous pagination), London,
    1967.

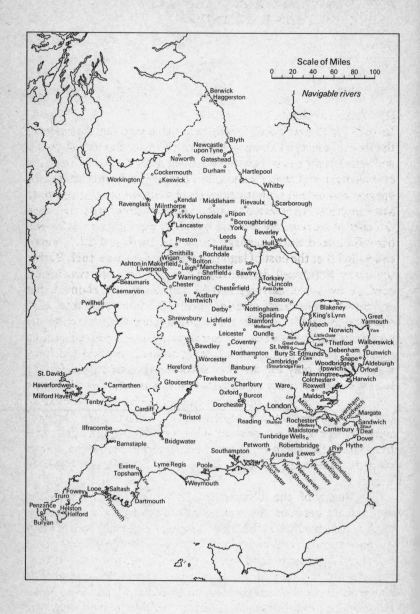

I THE MOVEMENT OF GOODS IN ELIZABETHAN ENGLAND

(1) *Land çarriage*

In 1675 Sir Robert Southwell presented his views on transport to the Royal Society. Taking as his text 'the principal use of the sea and rivers is for easier carriage of commodities', he compared the cost of land and water carriage. Though his figures cannot be verified and indeed are not wholly consistent, his conclusions have some interest. He asserted that the 'ordinary proportion' between the cost of carriage by sea and by wheel carriage was 1:20, and between inland water carriage and wheel carriage 1:12. Thus he concluded that the cost of land to water carriage was 16:1. Rather unusually Southwell divided land carriage into its two forms, carriage by wheel carriage and by horseback. He claimed that carriage by horseback accounted for 60 per cent of total land carriage although it was one-third dearer than carriage by wagon.[1] Though little reliance can be placed on Southwell's actual figures, his analysis of relative costs of different forms of transport was valid not only for the later seventeenth century but for the later sixteenth century as well. Indeed it was valid for all periods until the coming of the railways adjusted the balance in favour of land carriage. Before that adjustment all forms of land transport were expensive in comparison with water transport. That was true during Elizabeth I's reign when the movement of goods was strongly influenced by the relative costs of different forms of transport.

The heart of the Elizabethan transport problem was the relationship between the weight and bulk of goods on the one hand and their value on the other. This was especially true of long-distance transport. Weighty and bulky goods of low value could not stand the cost of land carriage over long distances, but they could stand the cost of water carriage, especially by sea. The classic example of this is coal, which could be shipped from Newcastle to London, but could not be carried far by land when the cost of land carriage doubled the pit-head price every ten miles or so. Weighty and bulky goods of high value, on the other hand, could stand the cost of expensive land carriage even over long distances. The classic examples of this are cloth and wool. Naturally the same was true for goods of low weight or bulk and high value such as spices and drugs or silk thread and silver buttons. Obviously goods of high value might go by water where that was possible and convenient, but equally obviously that was often not possible and was sometimes not convenient. In such cases there was the alternative of road transport, either by wagon or pack-horse.

Very little is known about roads and land transport in this period, and very little may ever be known. It would seem that there was an interest in land routes with their stages and distances, more especially the routes radiating from London. Printed road tables began to appear in 1541, not as separate publications but as appendices to 'chronicles'. The earliest of these tables gives nine roads to London from Walsingham, Berwick, Caernarvon, Cockermouth, Great Yarmouth, Dover, St Buryan, Bristol and St Davids. By 1570 these had been augmented by roads from Southampton, Nottingham, Lincoln, Boston, Carmarthen, Cambridge, Oxford and Rye. By then, too, the cross roads were appearing in the tables.[2] William Smith, whose 'Particular description of England' was dated 1588 but not published until the nineteenth century, listed more than a dozen cross-country roads. These included a batch radiating from Bristol to Oxford, Cambridge, Southampton, Shrewsbury and Chester. Smith also included distances between places when he was describing particular towns (rather in the manner of a motorist's handbook). Thus he described Blackburn as seven miles from Preston, and the entry for Wigan runs 'Wigan is 7 myles southwest from Bolton, and standeth uppon the head of the river Dowles, which falleth into the mouth of the Ribble'.[3] The compilers of these road tables seem to have copied from one another. They all underestimated distances by using a computed mile which seems to have been between a third and a quarter longer than the statute mile. This difference should be borne in mind when dealing with contemporary references to mileage. Thus the post was supposed to travel at 7 miles per hour in summer and 5 miles per hour in winter,[4] but did people think of this in terms of a computed or of a statute mile? It is possible that these early road lists were compiled as a guide to the post routes and stages, rather than as a general guide for travellers or carriers. Whatever their purpose, they throw no light on the condition of roads or on the goods that the roads carried.

Nothing else throws very much light on the condition of roads either. The responsibility for repairing roads was laid on the parishes by the well-known Act of 1555, which provided for the appointment of two surveyors of highways in each parish. The men of the parish were to work for four days on the roads each year. They were to work an eight-hour day, which seems to be a very early example of what was to become a traditional working day.[5] This statute labour was unpaid and was raised to six days a year in 1563.[6] All this is familiar enough, but the results of it are hard to determine. It is not known how seriously parishes took their responsibility or how far statute labour was enforced. By the early seventeenth century, when quarter sessions records become more abundant, many parishioners clearly preferred to pay their fines rather than work on the roads. The money so raised by fines was presumably used to hire labour for road work, which may have been a more efficient system than the annual jamboree of reluctant statute labourers. What work was actually done on the roads it is impossible to say. Surveyors had the right to take stone and gravel, and there was some provision for keeping ditches open for carrying away water from roads. This need for drainage was strongly emphasised in Thomas Procter's work of 1607 and 1610, which in a crude way anticipates the views of the eighteenth-century road engineers.[7] But it is doubtful whether any of the parish surveyors read Procter.

Though we do not know much about the condition of Elizabethan highways (to use the contemporary term), we can detect an increased interest in them and their use. This is reflected in the publication of road tables with their detailed stages and inaccurate distances. It is reflected, too, in the new administrative system of parochial responsibility for road maintenance and in the continued bequests of money for the repair of roads and bridges. As with poor relief, private benevolence supplemented parochial action. Such an interest would be natural in a society of great geographical mobility. People as well as goods moved along the roads. A stream of boys from all over the country converged on London where they took up their apprenticeship in the city companies. By 1621 'an ydle custom' had arisen in London 'that all Cheshire men about this towne, Staffordshire men, Northampton, Sussex, Suffolke (*et sic de caeteris*) shold have a meeting once a yeare at some hall and layeng their monie together have a feast', which 'must not be don without a sermon'.[8] There were similar, if smaller, migrations to provincial towns like Bristol and Shrewsbury. Men and boys were more mobile than goods; at the very worst they could follow the example of cattle and walk. But goods moved along the roads too. Perhaps historians of transport, with their outlook of suburban motorists, are too concerned with the condition of the roads and too obsessed with Arthur Young's ruts four feet deep (which must have been made by wheels about nine feet in diameter). Much land transport was by pack-horse which needed a track rather than a road. Even wheeled vehicles when drawn by horses can travel along surprisingly bad roads. Within living memory the dirt roads of the Canadian prairies, which somewhat resembled Elizabethan highways, were passable by horse-drawn wagons when rain had rendered them impassable for motor vehicles even with chains. Moreover, given the size of the Elizabethan population and the nature of the Elizabethan economy with its wide dispersal of agriculture and industry, it was plainly impossible for the roads to have been 'good' in the modern sense. Such a population and such an economy needed a network of roads which would be usable, but which in practice, even with a considerable movement of people and goods, would be lightly used in comparison with modern roads. To have brought, or to have tried to bring, such roads up to a high standard might well have been a waste of economic resources and might not have reduced the cost of transport appreciably. Land carriage by horses is inherently expensive for much the same reason that the production of goods under a domestic system is expensive in comparison with factory production. In both cases the unit of production is small, it is very labour-intensive and there is no economy of scale. Indeed two things seem clear about Elizabethan roads, though neither can be proved satisfactorily by statistics; they are that the carriage of goods on such roads was rather expensive and that it was also extensive.

Transport costs are more difficult to determine than wages or commodity prices in this period; in the scale of difficulty they rank with urban rents or with costs of production of manufactured goods. It is a question of evidence; the sources produce only scattered examples and even these may be difficult to interpret in terms of weight and distance. There are two ways of assessing transport costs according to the evidence available. The first is the rather crude method of comparing the cost of carriage with the price or value of the goods carried. This is really all that can be done when the weight of the goods is not known. The second and more satisfactory method is to work out the cost of carriage in ton-miles. This obviously requires knowledge of the weight of the goods, the distance covered and the amount paid for carriage. Such information is not very readily available.

Both these methods of assessing transport costs can be illustrated from the Shuttleworth accounts which, down to 1599, record the carriage of goods to and from Smithills near Bolton in Lancashire. Thus in September 1589 ling and cod bought for £1 9s 9d at Stourbridge fair cost 10s in carriage to Smithills, thus adding about a third to the purchase price,[9] but in 1595 ling costing £2 paid only 8s in carriage.[10] These were long hauls; in contrast, wine bought at Chester in May 1592 for £13 11s 2d cost 9s 4d in carriage to Smithills,[11] and 19 gallons 1 quart of wine bought at Manchester in 1594 for £1 10s 6d cost only 9d in carriage.[12] Such examples are not very illuminating. Nor are the statements that the carriage of a pack from London to Smithills cost anything from 6s to 11s.[13] It is more interesting to learn that 'Panter the carrier' was paid £1 13s 4d in July 1589 as 'the reste of the monye which was unpayed for the carredge of a wane-lode of stuffe from London'. To those who think that wheeled carriage as well as civilisation stopped at the Trent, it might be supposed that 'wane-lode' was simply a unit of capacity, but one Frampolde was paid 3d 'for wachinge the wane which was frachted [freighted] with stuffe which came from Londone'.[14]

The more satisfactory method of working out transport charges in terms of cost per ton-mile can be used in only a few cases from entries in the Shuttleworth accounts. Thus in November 1586 a carrier was paid 6s for the carriage 'of a hundrethe, savinge a quarteron, of hoppes', apparently from London, which gives a rate of about 10d a ton-mile.[15] Six months later another carrier, Lawrence Fogge, charged 1s for taking six puddings (were they black?) to London; they weighed 16 lb, so that the rate was about 8·6d a ton-mile.[16] In August 1589 yet another carrier, John Page, brought $10\frac{1}{2}$ cwt of unspecified goods from London to Smithills for £2 17s 9d, or 6·6d a ton-mile.[17] More local transport seems to have been rather cheaper. In June 1590 $\frac{3}{4}$ ton of iron bought at Chester for £10 13s 8d, cost 11s 4d in carriage to Smithills, or 5d a ton-mile;[18] in May 1593 a ton of Spanish iron, bought at Liverpool for £12, cost 10s 4d in carriage to Smithills, or 4·3d a ton-mile.[19]

These wide variations in cost per ton-mile are a feature of the period. Thorold Rogers thought the range was from 3d to over 6d a ton-mile, but his own examples of land carriage between Oxford and London and Cambridge and London show much higher rates, from 8·9d to 11·4d a ton-mile. Between London and Wormleighton in 1600–2 they were higher still, being from $10\frac{1}{2}d$ to 1s $2\frac{3}{4}d$ a ton-mile.[20] Rates may have varied according to the time of the year. On 3 March 1623 Marie Coke of Hall Court, Much Marcle in Herefordshire, informed her husband, John Coke, that the wain carrier of Dymock had enquired whether he could carry Coke's stuff to London, saying that his usual rates were 6s cwt before May, 5s cwt after May to midsummer and 4s to 4s 6d from midsummer to Michaelmas.[21] These rates give a seasonal range of 8d to 1s a ton-mile. It is difficult to tell whether seasonal rates were charged in the sixteenth century; there seems to be no evidence that they were. Rates may have varied according to the size of the consignment, with small parcels being relatively more expensive. Thus in 1588 a parcel weighing 28 lb was carried from London to Huddersfield for 4s 8d, which works out at the very high rate of 2s a ton-mile.[22] This looks like a flat rate of 2d lb between London and Huddersfield, which does not make it any less expensive. Flat rates per pound were certainly used for through journeys. In the 1560s and 1570s the Mines Royal at Keswick made use of the Stable family as their land carriers between Keswick and London. The charge was always 1d a pound, which works out at about 8d a ton-mile. This flat rate was charged regardless of the nature or size of the load; six Dutch chairs packed in mats and weighing 2 cwt, or five casks of assay crucibles weighing 326 lb, or 278 lb of groceries were all brought from London at 1d lb. Similarly 25 lb of copper pots were carried to London for 2s 1d.[23] The carriers also took passengers from London to Keswick at 16s 8d a head, but this seems to mean that the passengers rode on horses provided by the carriers who escorted them. Thus in December 1571 one of the Stables was paid £3 6s 8d for taking two smelters and their wives to Keswick with four horses. The following year another carrier, Roger Jackson, was paid £10 for taking the Hochstetter family from London to Keswick, but they travelled by carriage.[24] The Mines Royal got goods by land from Workington and Newcastle as well as from London. Thus iron was brought from Workington to Keswick at 8.6d a ton-mile in 1569 and from Newcastle at 6d a ton-mile in the same year.[25]

The cost of land carriage normally lay within the range of 4d to 12d a ton-mile. Almost all the examples that can be found fall within this range, whether they are cheese from Wayhill to Winchester at 8½d to 10d a ton-mile, or sugar from London to Winchester at 7·4d a ton-mile,[26] or books, close stools and other goods from London to Grafton Manor near Bromsgrove at 6·1d a ton-mile.[27] This range is too great to be very informative, but in fact there was some grouping of rates within the 6d to 9d range. In theory rates should have increased in sympathy with the rising prices of the period. There is some very slight indication of this, but the evidence is too meagre and too conflicting to support any firm correlation between transport costs and the general price index.

However we look at the figures, we get the impression that land carriage was expensive. This impression is heightened by any comparison between land and water carriage. Water carriage, whether by river or sea, was normally much cheaper than land carriage. There are some striking examples of this. In 1588 when the building of the manor house at Kyre in Worcestershire was begun, stone was quarried at Madeley in Shropshire and brought down the Severn to Bewdley and then by land to Kyre. Carriage down the river cost a little more than 1d a ton-mile, but the land carriage was 8d to 9d a ton-mile.[28] In the same year Magdalen College, Oxford, obtained one hundred salt fish from London; the carriage by water from London to Burcot was 7s, but the carriage by land for the eight miles from Burcot to Oxford was 2s. In 1599 wainscots were carried from London to Burcot by the Thames for a little over 1d a ton-mile; even allowing for the extra distance by water, this was cheap transport.[29] The contrast between the cost of carriage by land and by sea could be even greater. The Mines Royal obtained some of their supplies by sea from London to

Newcastle and then by land from Newcastle to Keswick. In 1569 they got $11\frac{1}{2}$ tons of malmsey wine from London; the carriage by sea to Newcastle was £2 6s, unlading and bridge tolls at Newcastle cost £1 9s 4d, and carriage from Newcastle to Keswick by cart £32 0s 2d. Similarly 15 tons of claret and French wine cost £3 in freight to Newcastle, £11 5s in carriage by cart to Barnard Castle, and £21 from Barnard Castle to Keswick. With other expenses, including drinks to the carriers, the total cost of getting the $26\frac{1}{2}$ tons of wine from London to Keswick was £77 17s 5d, of which about £6 16s represented the cost of water carriage. In the same year 8 tons of iron were shipped from London to Newcastle for £1 (perhaps 0·1d a ton-mile) and carted to Keswick for £20.[30] These very low freight rates by sea may be exceptional; the colliers returned from London to Newcastle in ballast and must have been ready to take in any cargo at almost any price. Certainly the cost of carriage from Newcastle to London seems to have been higher than in the reverse direction. It was 7s ton for copper in 1573 and about 8s 7d ton, also for copper, in 1576.[31] But for a voyage of perhaps three hundred miles this was hardly expensive.

Though land carriage appears expensive, especially in comparison with carriage by water, there is no doubt that goods were extensively transported by land. This can best be illustrated by looking at the woollen cloth trade. The manufacture of cloth was the largest industry in the country and it was widely dispersed. Moreover cloth so dominated the export trade that no other export was of much significance. Finally most of the cloth was exported through London. These simple facts show that there must have been a great movement of cloth, especially to London. Cloth was carried by land or by water or by a combination of the two. One of the most impressive examples of land carriage is provided by the Kendal pack-horse men who took cloth to Southampton and returned with such imported goods as raisins and figs, madder and woad, alum and canvas. The round trips took just over a month, and it is significant that they were undertaken in winter as well as in summer. Some Yorkshire and Lancashire pack-horse men also carried cloth to Southampton. This trade with Southampton declined in the second half of the sixteenth century.[32] Perhaps some of it was diverted to London. In 1618 John Lowden, a chapman of Stratford-le-Bow, left £60 to establish a fund for granting loans to six of the poorest carriers plying between Kendal and London or Wakefield and London, adding somewhat sourly, 'provided that they be not Lancashire men'.[33] Cloth might go by river, as the Norwich cloth that was sent down the Yare to Great Yarmouth; or it might go by sea, as Carmarthen and Milford sent frieze to Bristol. Or there might be a combination of land and river transport or land and sea. In June 1570 two Manchester clothiers, Miles Wilson and Roger Saule, sent northern kerseys and Manchester cottons to Bewdley, obviously by land, for shipment down the Severn to Bristol.[34] Two more Manchester clothiers, George and Charles Travis, sent packs of linen and woollen cloth to Gloucester in 1592, again for shipment to Bristol.[35]

The case of Sandwich in 1580 is more curious. A Port Book for that year records not only the coastwise shipments from Sandwich but also goods sent by land. It shows that Sandwich shipped to London quantities of cloth (Hasbrough linen, bustian, cambric, bombasines, Bruges fustian), Bruges thread, hemp, teazels and ten dozen fans. It also sent to London by road the same sorts of cloth, together with says, rash, canvas, cantelet lace, incle, raw silk and thirteen and a half dozen ruffs, fifteen dozen and nine handkerchiefs and a dozen cauls. Most of these goods had probably been imported into Sandwich before being passed on to London, but it is not clear why they should have gone by sea one week and by land the next. Quantities of cantelet lace, crewel fringe and yarn, Bruges thread, caddas and incle were sent to Canterbury by land, but that was more understandable; the land route was much more direct than the river route by the Stour (assuming it was navigable).[36] Thus cloth could travel by a variety of means, but there is no doubt that most of it went by land as a glance at the London export trade suggests.

In the three years 1586–8 London exported an annual average of 106,000 notional shortcloths.[37] These cloths were not made in London, though a very few may have been dyed and dressed there. They were made in the cloth-producing areas and sent to London for export. There is no evidence that any of them reached London by river; no evidence, for example, that west country cloth found its way to the Thames and was carried downstream to the capital by the western bargemen or that Suffolk cloth found its way to the Lea and so into the Thames. Some cloth certainly reached London by sea. The London Port Book for Michaelmas 1585 to

Michaelmas 1586 shows shipments of cloth to London from Berwick, Hull, Great Yarmouth, Aldeburgh, Woodbridge, Ipswich and Colchester. In no cases were the shipments large, and some of the cloths—sackcloth from Woodbridge, Aldeburgh and Ipswich, dornix from Great Yarmouth for example—were not woollen cloth and would not figure among London's export of shortcloths.[38] It is rash to generalise from limited evidence, but the Port Books for provincial ports show very little woollen cloth going to London. One could hazard a guess that 100,000 out of the 106,000 shortcloths exported from London had reached the capital by land. Moreover this figure takes no account of cloth sent to London for consumption there or for re-distribution by land or by the coasting trade. This is difficult to estimate. Dr Jones's tentative estimate for 1583–5, based on the hallage receipts, implies that more cloth was sent to London for consumption there than was exported from London.[39] Given London's population, this seems unlikely, unless in fact some of the cloth was not consumed in London but re-distributed. The London Port Book for 1585–6 suggests that London shipped more woollen cloth by the coast to places like Ipswich, Great Yarmouth, Dover, Sandwich, Faversham, Walberswick, Woodbridge and Maidstone than it received by the coast. Much of this cloth was probably exported from these provincial ports. In the mid 1580s there was concern over the carriage of cloth by land from London to other ports where, it was alleged, much was exported without paying duty.[40] It is difficult to believe that it was worth carrying cloth by land to avoid a duty of 6s 8d a cloth, but if it were, it might be even more profitable to send it by the cheaper sea route.

Whether we assume that 100,000 notional shortcloths were sent to London by land for export or 200,000 or more were sent for export and local consumption, either way it involved a good deal of land carriage. The smaller number of cloths should have weighed about 2,700 tons; this was perhaps equivalent to 27,000 journeys by one indefatigable pack-horse, or one journey by 27,000 less energetic pack-horses. Much cloth had to go by land if it were to go at all, but some went by land where it could have gone by water. Thus, Norwich cloth might go down the Yare to Great Yarmouth for export, but it did not take that route to London. It took the more direct land route to the capital. The Welsh cloth that was carried from Oswestry to Shrewsbury to be dressed did not reach the London export market by going down the Severn and round the south coast. This is hardly surprising in view of the difference in distance between the land and water routes. But in March 1598 when Shrewsbury corporation was buying grain for the relief of the poor, it bought wheat, barley and rye from Thomas Oxwick of Walsingham in Norfolk and arranged for them to be shipped by sea to Bristol and then up the Severn.[41] Norfolk cloth would not have taken that route.

Though cloth could stand the cost of land carriage, in real terms that cost must have varied greatly with the distance covered and with the quality of the cloth, even though the cheaper cloth was usually lighter in weight. Thus in the 1560s John Isham was buying 'checked carssis' in Halifax at 10s a kersey. There should have been 112 kerseys, costing £56, to the ton. We do not know the cost of their carriage to London, but at 1s a ton-mile it would be about £9 13s. Perhaps the rate was lower, for Isham along with other London merchants preferred the land route to the river and sea route.[42] Perhaps, too, one of the advantages of land carriage, as with modern road haulage, was that it could be door-to-door. The alternative route from Halifax would have involved sending the cloth by land to the Ouse, by river boat to Hull, by coasting ship to London and perhaps by lighter from the ship to the London wharf. The cost of land carriage fell less heavily on the more expensive cloths. A long broadcloth weighed as much as four kerseys, but its value was more than four times that of a kersey.[43] Costly imported fabrics must often have reached the consumer by land, but of their movement inland from the ports we know little. We know little, too, about the movement of home-produced linen, but the Lancashire linen industry certainly distributed its products widely by land.[44]

Land carriage was ubiquitous and important, more important than many suppose, yet little can be discovered about its organisation and methods. Often it is difficult to tell whether goods were going by pack-horse or by wagon or cart; nor is it clear how much a pack-horse or wagon or cart normally carried. A standard work on transport assures us that 'a packhorse could carry no more than about $2\frac{1}{2}$ cwt'; and later tells us that 'pack-horses or mules, each carrying five or six hundredweights, could form caravans capable of crossing the wildest country.'[45] The Webbs believed that horses could carry half a ton if they were 'fine, strapping, broad-chested Lincolnshire animals'.[46] Some of these estimates seem far too high, at least for the sixteenth century. At Keswick, where the Mines Royal employed a vast amount of local transport, the horse-load was just under 2 cwt.[47] When the Shuttleworths brought 3 cwt 9½ lb of iron from Halifax to Burnley in 1600, they described it as two horse-loads.[48] This would make the horse-load just under 1½ cwt, but that may not have been a full load. In other words, 3 cwt 9½ lb may have been too much for one horse, so two had to be used. A horse-load of coal seems to have been just over 2 cwt.[49] The evidence is hardly conclusive, but it suggests that a pack-horse carried about 2 cwt. If that were so, it would require ten pack-horses to carry a ton, which was the weight two horses could draw in a cart. Perhaps this was the basis of Southwell's view that carriage by horseback was dearer than by wheeled carriage.

When John Taylor published his rather primitive directory of carriers in 1637, he listed the towns from which the carriers started for London, the London inns at which the carriers lodged and the day or days of the week on which they arrived or were 'to bee had' at the inn. He claimed to be covering 'carriers, waggons, foote-posts and higglers', but he did not clearly distinguish between carriers by wagon and by pack-horse.[50] Perhaps he thought the distinction irrelevant, as in a sense it was from his point of view. Whether Taylor's list was accurate or not, it clearly shows an extensive carrying service between provincial towns and London: a service based on regular schedules and established connections with London inns. Clearly too the service was not new. It is possible to find common carriers operating a service to London before 1637. In 1613, for example, the common carrier at Bury St Edmunds was to leave for London on a Monday and return by Saturday, for the better observance of the Sabbath.[51] A similar arrangement was made in 1599 at Ipswich, where there were two carriers with wagons plying regularly to London.[52] Even so, it is difficult to tell how widespread this regular service was in the sixteenth century. The Shuttleworths employed three named carriers plying between Lancashire and London, at least one of whom used a wain; another, Lawrence Fogge, was entrusted with £8 in August 1591 to buy spices in London. The spices were probably in a pack that cost 8s 6d in carriage from London to Manchester.[53] The carriage of packs, trunks, chests and specified goods between Smithills near Bolton and London does rather suggest a regular service. Similarly the two carriers, old Stable and young Stable, may have operated a regular service between Keswick and London. York, too, had its link with the capital. In 1586 Thomas Screven wrote to John Manners from London saying that he was sending a trunk with the York carrier. It contained, among other things, a gown with white satin sleeves, and the charge was 3s lb, which was so high as to make one suspect a mistake—or was it a special rate for a very valuable consignment?[54] Five years earlier York had decreed that William Yong, a boy, was to be paid 20s towards getting a master in the city; if he could not get one, he was to be newly apparalled and sent to London by carrier.[55] Presumably he was not charged at 3d lb. More interesting is the example of Chester where in 1580 it was reported to Lord Burghley that 'the carryers of Chester come wekely to Bosomes Inne in St Lorance Lane, where carriage may be had to this cyttie'.[56] This is much in the style of Taylor's directory, though Taylor usually gave the day of arrival in London. These random examples, which could be augmented, do not prove a great deal, but they suggest that an Elizabethan 'carriers' cosmography' could have been compiled.

Land carriage remains an obscure subject, but enough is known about it to show that it was an important element in the inland trade. Without it, the fairs and markets, the wholesalers and shopkeepers could not have functioned as they did. The frictions of distance were formidable, but they did not result in immobility. In the sixteenth century, when sources are scanty, land transport tends to be studied as an adjunct to other branches of the economy, to agriculture or industry or trade, just as corn-milling tends to be regarded as an adjunct to agriculture. Yet in a sense transport, like corn-milling, was an industry in its own right and presented some of the features common to other industries of the period. How far, for example, was land carriage a part-time occupation? Much local transport was probably of this nature, providing a by-industry for farmers as weaving might do. In 1600 the opponents of the scheme to improve and extend the navigation of the Medway claimed that it would lead to the decay of husbandry, for 'honest men' would be deprived of land carriage and so forced to sell their oxen. The supporters of the scheme replied that men were so greedy for land carriage that some sold their land to buy oxen, others used their land solely to keep oxen for transport, while others were engaged in land carriage when they should have been spreading manure or tilling their ground and even had to hire men to plough their land for them.[57] All this is rather analogous to the question whether a man was primarily a farmer and secondarily a textile worker or the reverse. Though local land carriage must often have been a part-time job, the regular services between provincial towns and London must have been operated by full-time carriers. The same is true of the long hauls, as between Kendal and Southampton, when men might be away for a month at a time. Even from London to Chester sixteen days were allowed for the carriage of gunpowder and arms by cart,[58] and the pack-horses carrying cloth from Shrewsbury to London had to leave on a Wednesday to arrive at Blackwell Hall on Thursday of the following week, which meant that, allowing for no travel on Sunday, they covered about twenty miles a day.[59] These were surely the journeys of professional carriers. Finally, where did all the horses come from? Those head-of-the-dale Yorkshire farms, which had little or no arable and carried many horses, suggest one source.[60] Doubtless there were many others, but the horse awaits its historian.

(2) River traffic

The difference in cost between road and river transport suggests that goods would be carried by water when that was possible and convenient. That may have been so, but river transport leaves very little evidence of its nature and extent. Just as it is difficult to determine the state of the roads, so it is difficult to determine the state of the rivers. How many of them were navigable, and what was the limit of navigation on individual rivers? The Elizabethans themselves did not give very helpful answers to these questions. William Smith, who seems to have had an interest in rivers as geographical features, listed the four principal rivers as the Thames, Severn, Humber and Trent. He did not say that either the Severn or the Humber was navigable. The Thames he thought was navigable to Dorchester, which was reasonable enough, though the head of navigation may have been Burcot. About the Trent he was more vague and more inaccurate; he thought it became navigable a little below its junction with the Sow, whereas in fact Nottingham was the head of navigation.[61] Here he was plainly guessing and guessing badly. William Harrison did not confine himself to the greater rivers but gave a long and tedious description of every river, rivulet and brook that he could find.[62] He noted the fish but not the freight, and his aquatic antiquarianism is no great help. Nor is Camden's, though both he and Harrison give an occasional reference to navigation. What is lacking is an Elizabethan Defoe.

The five major rivers, the Yorkshire Ouse, the Trent, the Great Ouse, the Thames and the Severn, were all tidal and therefore passage along them, within the tidal limits, was free and common to all. They were all navigable but, except for the Severn, very little is known about the goods they carried. It is even doubtful whether intensive local research would reveal very much about the traffic on some of these rivers. The absence of tolls removed any incentive to record the passage of goods. Later, when the improvement of rivers led to the imposition of tolls to pay for the improvement, records of such tolls must have been kept, but they do not survive before the end of the seventeenth century. Traffic on the Severn is better documented simply because Gloucester ranked as a seaport and so its trade was recorded in the Port Books.

The tidal limit of the Yorkshire Ouse was York, which had once ranked as a seaport but which, by the second half of the sixteenth century, had become purely a river port.[63] The increased size of ships and perhaps some deterioration in the river prevented sea-going vessels from reaching the city. Thus goods passing down the river had to be transhipped at Hull if they were to be exported or go by the coast; similarly sea-borne goods entering Hull were transhipped into keels for passage up the Ouse. Indeed this river traffic has to be deduced largely from a study of Hull's trade. There is no doubt that lead was shipped down the Ouse,[64] and little doubt that it was joined by grain, cloth and perhaps butter. The upward cargoes must have been more varied. The evidence of Hull's trade suggests that they included coal (originally from Newcastle), wine, raw materials of the cloth industry (oil, madder, woad, alum) and haberdashery, groceries and upholsterers' wares (originally from London). Certainly some of the goods from London were recorded in the names of York merchants and tradesmen.[65] To this list should be added iron, salt, clapboard and wainscot, pitch, tar, ashes and fish (including herrings and stockfish); all these appear among the goods carried in the Ouse keels.[66]

The exact geographical extent of this river traffic is difficult to determine. The Ouse was navigable to York, but York itself is sometimes represented as the centre of a network of water communication by the Ouse, Swale and Ure.[67] There is little evidence of this, though there was some river traffic between York and Boroughbridge, and Harrison certainly described the Foss, which flows into the Ouse at York, as 'able to beare a good vessell'.[68] Others have extended this water transport even further. According to Professor Stone, iron from the Earl of Rutland's iron works at Rievaulx 'had ready water transport from Rievaulx to Hull and from Hull to London', and this made large sales possible 'by breaking into the London market'.[69] As Rievaulx appears to have been distant from any water transport, it would be interesting to know what route the iron took. Below York neither the Wharfe nor the Aire seems to have been navigable, though both may have had some traffic on their lower reaches; the Don at this time had no direct access to the Ouse. Lower down still, the river Hull and Beverley Beck gave Hull a navigable channel to Beverley. The Beck was 'a creek digged with man's hand'.[70] Its medieval origin is obscure; according to Camden it was made by the townsmen,[71] and certainly the corporation of Beverley spent considerable sums in scouring it.[72] The traffic it bore can only be guessed at, except for the Londoners' goods (grocery, haberdashery and mercery wares) which were sent for the famous Cross Fair in May. The Fair was attended by York as well as London merchants. Towards the end of May 1574 Hull was shipping to London grocery, haberdashery and mercery wares.[73] Had they failed to find a buyer at the Fair? This penetration by water into the East Riding was unimportant compared with Hull's access southwards by the Trent.

The Trent is often regarded as a boundary, a sort of water curtain between two cultures, but it was an important channel of communication. It had certainly not been 'digged by man's hand', but it was often obstructed by man's handiwork in the form of 'wears, mills, pales and kidells'. In 1593 Sir Thomas Stanhope's weir at Shelford was attacked by what was alleged to be a 'rent-a-mob', or in the language actually used, 'certen persons purpozelie hired from sondrie remote partes thereunto'.[74] Despite obstructions, the Trent was navigable to Nottingham, which it 'serveth aboundantly with fish' according to Camden,[75] who unfortunately was more interested in fish than in water transport. It seems impossible to get any picture of the traffic on the Trent. There is no doubt that coal from the Wollaton area was shipped down the river from Nottingham; indeed in the early seventeenth century there was even an abortive scheme to supply London with coal from Wollaton and Strelley.[76] According to later evidence the coal boats returned upstream with corn in times of scarcity,[77] but in normal times there was probably a downward traffic in corn. Later evidence would suggest, too, that timber was shipped down the Trent from Stockwith. Certainly Derbyshire lead was carried by land to Bawtry and then shipped down the Idle and Trent.[78] It is possible that cutlery and other metal goods from the Sheffield area took the same route. It is equally possible that iron went up the Trent and the Idle to Bawtry for the Sheffield cutlers, and that some of Hull's imports of wine, groceries and dyestuffs passed up the Trent to Nottingham. But in the present state of knowledge this is conjecture.

The Trent was an important river, but only one of its tributaries, the Idle, was navigable.[79] Another 'tributary', the Foss Dyke, was an artificial channel variously attributed to the Romans and to Henry I, which linked the Trent at Torksey with Lincoln. The Foss Dyke had been navigable but it seems to have deteriorated in the early sixteenth century when attempts to scour it were never completed. By 1571 Lincoln was complaining of a shortage of timber and proposing an Act of Parliament to set up a commission 'to assess all persons within seven miles of the city for the dyking, cleansing and scouring of Foss-dyke', by which timber could be brought by water from Nottinghamshire.[80] Nothing came of this project, but the Foss Dyke appears to have been navigable on occasion for Harrison wrote that 'in great floods vessells may come from Trents side to Lincolne'.[81] On such occasions it would have been possible to go from York to Lincoln by inland waterways, but it is doubtful whether any goods took that route.

Further south the Great Ouse opened up a vast area where drainage had always been considered as important as navigation and where the two were often in conflict. It was an area in which the natural courses of rivers had been radically altered by man and where the problem of navigation included the maintenance of an outfall to the sea. These complex problems of change and flow cannot be dealt with here.[82] The Ouse itself was navigable to St Ives; there is no clear evidence of even local traffic higher up the river. Of the tributaries, the Cam is known to have been navigable to Cambridge,[83] and there was some traffic on the Little Ouse and the Lark. This recital of traffic on the rivers familiar to the atlases of today does not do justice to the network of waterways that could be reached from King's Lynn. Thus the Ouse system was linked with the Nen at Wisbech, and the Nen itself was navigable to Peterborough, which was 'beautified with a "portable" river to bring and carry all merchantable commodities to five sundry shires adjoining upon it'.[84] A modern map illustrating the destinations of goods sent from King's Lynn after the February Mart of 1585 shows such goods going north to Boston, Sleaford and Lincoln, west to Spalding, Leicester, Stamford, Peterborough, Oundle, Northampton and St Ives, south to Cambridge, Newmarket and Ely and east to Thetford.[85] Though these 'loads' could not always go the whole way by water, their distribution is a good indication of the role of King's Lynn as a distributive centre. The goods carried on this complex of waterways cannot be established in detail, but the general picture is clear enough. That picture is dominated by the goods that were brought into or carried out of King's Lynn by sea. From the cargoes coming into King's Lynn by sea, coal was the most important commodity going up river. It was joined by wine, fish, salt, soap, iron and groceries. From the cargoes going out of King's Lynn by sea, much of the corn (chiefly wheat, malt, barley and rye) and the butter and cheese had reached the port by the river.[86] Basically perhaps it was an exchange of coal for corn, but that simplification hardly does justice to the role of water transport in the large region served by the Great Ouse.

Corn and coal may have dominated the river trade of the Thames too. The Thames was navigable to Burcot where goods were unloaded and carried by land to Oxford. There seems, however, to have been some local river traffic above Burcot. In 1581 the churchwardens of Stanford-in-the-Vale, Berkshire, paid 4d 'for brynging leade from Oxforde by botte',[87] which implies that a boat could pass from Oxford to Abingdon and then up the river Ock. Two years later Oxford City Council made orders about the unloading of boats with hay, wood, stone, slate and other goods at High Bridge in Oxford, which again implies navigation above Burcot.[88] Perhaps Burcot was the terminus for the great western barges, which were large sailing barges though on occasion they were towed by as many as three horses.[89] They carried down stream 'necessarie provision' for London,[90] which certainly included large quantities of grain. According to Camden, Henley was mostly inhabited by watermen, 'who make their chiefest gaine by carrying downe in their barges wood and corne to London'.[91] Coal must have gone upstream, but it has left little trace; nor has anything else left much trace except for the occasional shipment of salt fish and wainscot to Oxford.[92] The shipments of 'necessarie provision' down the Thames were supplemented by those down the Lea from Ware in Hertfordshire. The navigation of the Lea was improved under an Act of 1571. This led to violent opposition from land carriers, but they could not prevent the river from developing a great trade in malt, corn and flour with London.

The Thames, according to Harrison, was much superior to the Severn 'in length of course, bountie of water, and depth of channel', but the Severn was not inferior to the Thames in 'trade of merchandize, plentie of carriage, and store of all kind of fish'. The Severn was 'to be discommended' only for its openness in many places to the weather, 'whereby sundrie perils oft overtake such as fish or saile in small vessels on the same'.[93] To this might have been added the obstructions to navigation caused by weirs of which a formidable list was drawn up in 1575.[94] Despite these defects the Severn was one of the great rivers. At this time it was navigable as high as Shrewsbury where, in 1581, it was the setting for an elaborate pageant in honour of Sir Henry Sidney, Lord President of the Council in the Marches of Wales. When Sidney left Shrewsbury by boat he passed an island on which 'a band of music was stationed with certain of the scholars [of Shrewsbury School] apparelled in the guise of water nymphs with green willows on their heads'.[95] Whatever the boys thought, it was an appropriate gesture from the head of navigation. Below Shrewsbury was a string of river ports all the way to Bristol. Of these, Gloucester ranked as a seaport, at first as a 'creek' of Bristol and after 1580 as a head port with its own 'creeks'.

The trade of the Severn centred on Bristol, which fortunately recorded at least some of that trade in its Port Books. The two Books for 1570–1 give a picture of the trade at that time.[96] Bristol was sending up the Severn a wide variety of goods: wine, oil, iron, soap, raisins, woad, linen, canvas, drywares and upholstery wares, frieze, pitch and tar, brazil, tin, brass, hops and fish. They went to Berkeley, Frampton-on-Severn, Newnham, Gloucester, Tewkesbury, Worcester, Bewdley and Bridgnorth. The most important single item was almost certainly wine (gascon and sack). This and some of the other goods had been imported into Bristol from abroad, just as the tin had come from Cornwall and the frieze from South Wales. The trade down the river showed less variety; it was almost monopolised by barley malt, wheat and peas from Tewkesbury and Gloucester to Bristol. In addition Shrewsbury sent wool, Bridgnorth wool, honey, candles and wax, and Bewdley calf-skins, tallow, leather and cloth. The Port Books imply that the river ports, besides their trade with Bristol, had a coasting trade of their own. Tewkesbury, Gloucester and Gatcombe are recorded as sending large quantities of wheat and barley malt to the ports of Wales (as far as Caernarvon), Devon and Cornwall. This trade in agricultural produce down river, and wine, footstuffs, manufactured goods and raw materials up river was continued after 1571, but with some modifications. There was some increase in manufactured goods going down stream and some increase in raw materials coming up from Bristol.[97] Even so, Gloucester's trade in 1592–3 was very similar to that of twenty years earlier, with large shipments of malt predominating.[98] Whether the trade changed much or little, there is no doubt it was important to the economy of the Severn valley. It was probably more important than even the Port Books reveal, for there must have been local trade, in coal for example, which remains unrecorded. The Port Books for Bristol and Gloucester provide a rare glimpse of what river trade could really amount to in this period. If similar Books were available for other rivers, the whole subject of river transport would be transformed.

The five great rivers and their tributaries carried most of the river traffic of the country, but not quite all. The most important exception was perhaps the three rivers, the Yare, Waveney and Bure, that centred on Great Yarmouth. All three were navigable to some extent, but the most important was the Yare which was navigable from Great Yarmouth to Norwich. Such a link between a port and the second city in the land could hardly fail to be important. Yarmouth was shipping coal up the Yare in the fourteenth century,[99] and much of the coal it got from Newcastle in the sixteenth century was sent up the river to Norwich, which also received by the same route wine, imported foodstuffs, fish, alum and woad for the cloth industry, iron and tin, bricks and tiles. In return Norwich sent down river little but cloth. This was sent to Yarmouth for export, not for the London market, which was served by land carriage.[100] When the Jesuit, William Weston, landed with Ralph Emerson on the Norfolk coast in 1584, Emerson took their books by water to Norwich, 'the starting-place for the freight-waggons and carriers that take the merchandise of the district to London'. The books were sent by land to an inn in London and promptly seized there.[101] Elsewhere there is evidence of some river traffic. The Medway was navigable to Maidstone, and occasionally small boats could get as high as Yalding.[102] On the Rother there was some carriage of iron above Rye[103] and on the Arun some carriage above Arundel.[104] There may have been more of this local traffic than the records reveal.

This movement of goods by water depended largely on comparative cost. A horse can draw more than it can carry; it can draw very much more if the load is floating in water. Many of the developments in transport have aimed at the reduction of the frictions of distance in the literal sense of the reduction of physical friction: the wheeled cart instead of the sledge with runners, the wheels running on railed tracks instead of on the road surface, the load transferred to the less resistant water, and so perhaps on to the frictionless travel of outer space. River boats seem often to have been towed by men rather than horses, which require a firmer towpath, and often they carried sail, but whatever the method they were cheaper than land carriage. Yet this is difficult to prove statistically, chiefly because of the lack of evidence but partly because any calculation of cost per ton-mile has to be used with caution. English rivers meander with a mazy motion, sometimes down to a sunless sea, and the distance by river may be much greater than the distance by land. Burcot is said to be about ninety-six miles from London by the Thames and fifty-three miles by road. Even if this is allowed for, the examples already given of carriage on the Thames and Severn show that water carriage was much cheaper than land carriage.[105] This was true also of the

Yorkshire Ouse, where in 1562 the Merchant Adventurers Company of York and the keel owners agreed on the freight rates between York and Hull. Such rates included 2s 4d for a ton of iron or other merchandise, 2s 6d for a last of flax, pitch, tar, ashes and red herrings, 1s 8d for a pack of cloth and 1s 2d for a fodder of lead 'taken in at the crayne' or 1s 6d if the lead was 'beyng lightened', which presumably meant taken to the keel in a lighter.[106] All these rates were much lower than those for any possible land carriage. On the Trent it was said in 1605 that a ton of coal could be carried from Nottingham to Gainsborough for 3s and from Gainsborough to Hull for 2s.[107] The following year it was claimed that, if the Nen were made navigable from Alwalton to Oundle, goods could be carried by water for 3d a ton or load compared with 6d by land.[108] Such comparisons were a commonplace of seventeenth-century navigation schemes and they should be taken with a grain of salt, but there is no doubt of their underlying truth.

The cost advantage of water carriage would suggest that efforts would be made to extend that carriage either by improving the already navigable parts of rivers or by making unnavigable rivers, or parts of rivers, navigable. Such efforts were made in this period, but they were not very numerous and not always successful. The reasons for this remain obscure. They do not seem to have been technical; the practice of 'cleansing' rivers by removing shoals and other obstructions was known, and so too was the use of the cut and the pound lock for improving navigation. The reasons seem to have been administrative and financial rather than technical. The Tudors sometimes used old administrative agencies for new tasks; thus they put the increasing burden of economic regulation onto the shoulders of the justices of the peace. The old agency for dealing with rivers was the Commission of Sewers, but that was concerned primarily with drainage and not with navigation. Its work might, of course, incidentally benefit navigation and in some cases might do so intentionally. Thus a Commission of Sewers at Shrewsbury in 1575 ordered the removal of trees along the towing paths on the ground that they interfered with the tow ropes, and ordered the alteration or destruction of weirs where they interfered with navigation.[109] But this was a special case, for there was statutory authority for the Commission's action on the Severn.[110] There is no doubt that a Commission of Sewers had no power to make navigable a river or part of a river that was not navigable. In 1600 some members of a Commission of Sewers wanted to extend the navigation of the Medway above Maidstone, but they were defeated. Even though there was some slight river traffic above Maidstone, the river there remained the private property of the riparian landowners, and a Commission of Sewers could not take away their rights.[111] That was the crux of the matter. To make a river navigable required a right of access, a right of passage and a right to acquire land for works on the river. Such rights could only be acquired by consent of the riparian landowners, which was difficult to achieve, or by royal grant or by Act of Parliament.

There were precedents for improving rivers under powers granted by Act of Parliament, but very little use was made of such Acts in Elizabeth's reign, when there were only two. In 1571 an Act of Parliament was passed for making the Welland navigable from Stamford to the sea. It was passed at the request of the aldermen, burgesses and commonalty of Stamford, who drew a graphic picture of 'the pytifull sighte' presented by the decayed buildings and decayed trade of their town, which used to be inhabited 'by a number of sondrie welthie and notable marchauntes'. Now the staple of wool had been lost because of the making of cloth and the ancient course and passage of the river had been altered and diverted for the erection of six or seven watermills between Stamford and Market Deeping. By the Act the Lord Chancellor or Lord Keeper could at any time, on the request of Stamford, grant a Commission or a Commission of Sewers to approved persons to make the river navigable either in its ancient course or by a new cut and to remove mills if necessary.[112] There was no mention of who was to pay for the work, and in fact no action was taken under the Act. The second Act was more successful. It was also passed in 1571 and was 'for the brynging of the Ryver of Lee to the northside of the citie of London'. The Lea was to be brought to London by a cut made at the expense of the lord mayor, commonalty and citizens of London. The part of the river between Ware and the new cut was to be cleansed at the 'costes and charges of the countrey'. This was a much more sophisticated Act than the one for the Welland for it set up a body of commissioners to determine the price to be paid for land and the compensation to be paid to millowners whose mills were injured by the cut.[113] Moreover the Act was carried out.

The cut was duly dug at a cost, it is sometimes said, of £80,000.[114] Thus use of the artificial cut was known, and so too was the pound lock. The short canal at Exeter, built in the 1560s under powers granted by an Act of 1539, had pound locks. This canal started just below Exeter and ran for about three miles before rejoining the river. It could only carry small boats, and so goods had to be transhipped into or out of sea-going ships at Topsham.[115] Despite its defects, the Exeter canal is rightly regarded as something of a landmark in the development of inland navigation.

Though the extension of river navigation may not have been retarded by technical difficulties, it may well have been retarded by the opposition of riparian landowners and millowners and by the failure to devise a satisfactory method of financing river improvements. Such improvements were regarded as public works to be financed by the locality. Thus in 1592 the Privy Council ordered the Kentish justices of the peace to put in execution an Act of 1515 for making the Kentish Stour navigable to Fordwich. As Canterbury could not bear the whole cost, it was to be levied on the county as a whole.[116] This was not necessarily a very popular method of financing. Only in the next century was it realised that undertakers, suitably authorised by Letters Patent or Act of Parliament, would finance a river improvement scheme in return for a monopoly of carriage on the river or simply the right to take tolls. Until that was realised, river improvements were limited in scope, as they were in Elizabeth's reign. Considering the wide use of patents of monopoly in other fields, it is rather surprising that they were not used in river improvement schemes at this time as they were in the first half of the seventeenth century. All this meant that river transport was largely confined to rivers that were naturally navigable. In a sense this was the first stage of river transport. In the second stage other rivers, including the tributaries of the great rivers, were made navigable. This created a number of separate systems of inland navigation. The final stage was to link these systems by canals, which was the real breakthrough. It is sometimes said that the linking of the Thames and the Severn was proposed in Elizabeth's reign, but there is no real proof of this. It was certainly proposed in the early seventeenth century.

Although the Elizabethans did not do very much to extend their river navigation, they possessed a basic framework of navigable waterways which rested largely on the greater rivers. These penetrated deeply into the country and so made water carriage available over considerable areas. There is no doubt that such water carriage was important in the movement of goods, even if it is impossible to measure it. The evidence suggests that many types of goods were carried by water, but that water carriage was especially important for bulky commodities. These obviously included coal and probably timber. By an Act of 1559 large trees were not to be converted into charcoal for making iron if they grew within fourteen miles of the Thames, Severn, Wye, Humber, Dee, Tyne, Tees and Trent or any other river or creek 'by the whiche carriage ys commonly used by boate or other vessell to any parte of the sea'.[117] This was meant to preserve large timber for ship-building, and the fourteen miles may have represented one day's haul of such timber by land. It is not clear whether large timber was simply floated downstream or carried by boat, but rafts, which seem to have been used on the Severn, may have been for the carriage of timber.[118] Corn, too, was an important river cargo, but there was much land carriage of corn in regions where there was no navigable water and also in bringing the corn to the rivers. The corn that passed down the Lea to London had been brought to the river by land. Finally there was wine, all of which was imported and therefore had to be distributed inland from the ports. Wine was a cumbersome thing to carry by land; unless it was moved in small quantities it needed wheeled carriage.[119] In 1633 when the price of wine was fixed by proclamation it was stated that, when wine had to be carried more than ten miles by land from the nearest port, an additional charge of £4 ton or 1*d* quart could be made for every thirty miles of land carriage, over and above the original ten miles.[120] This type of allowance went back to the fourteenth century.[121] Though wine was, and had to be, carried by land, it was usually obtained from the nearest point to which it could be brought by water. Thus the Shuttleworths got their wine in bulk from Chester and Liverpool, though they also obtained small quantities in Manchester.[122] John Talbot of Grafton Manor near Bromsgrove got some of his at Worcester, to which, no doubt, it had come up the river from Bristol.[123] This tapping of water carriage at the nearest available point must have been common to many goods. It is a reminder that land and water carriage were often interdependent.

(3) The coasting trade

Thanks to the existence of the Port Books, the coasting trade is the best-documented branch of the inland trade. There is, however, no full and detailed study of the Elizabethan coasting trade, though work, some of it unpublished, has been done on individual ports or groups of ports. Here it is proposed only to give a general sketch of the trade, based on that work and on a sample of the Port Books. No doubt such a sketch will be amended and corrected by later work by other hands. The coasting trade was an integral part of the internal trade of the country, and its connection with other branches of that trade is obvious. Navigable rivers had ports at or near their mouths from which goods, which had been brought down river, could be shipped coastwise and from which other goods, originally brought in coasting ships, could be carried up river. Where such ports had no water communication with their hinterlands, goods were brought to or carried from the ports by land, which was the case with most south coast and some east coast ports. At Ipswich earlier in the century, Henry Tooley distributed imported goods, including wine and fish, over a wide area by land.[124] The need for this sort of distribution by land would have been greater had it not been for England's long and indented coastline and the great number of ports, creeks and havens that dotted the coast. The Port Books record the trade of some eighty-six ports and creeks, and there may have been other, less official, ones.[125] Much of the coasting trade was concentrated in about a quarter of these ports and creeks, and a good deal of it was concentrated in London.

In a very crude sort of way London's position in the coasting trade can be illustrated by the size of the Port Books recording that trade. A London Port Book covering the coasting trade for a year could run to ninety-five folios, or about three times the size of that of any provincial port. Yet the nature of the coasting trade made it impossible for London to dominate that trade as it did the country's foreign trade. London's foreign trade was greater than that of all the provincial ports put together, but its coasting trade was by definition part of the coasting trade of those ports. In a purely theoretical situation where the provincial ports traded only with London, London's coasting trade would be equal to that of the provincial ports, but it could never be greater. This is not, of course, to deny that London exercised great influence on the volume, nature and direction of the trade of individual ports. That was inevitable given a capital city that was the greatest port in the country and was ten times as populous as the biggest provincial town.

It is easier to analyse the goods going to London by the coast than it is to analyse the goods distributed from London. This is just the reverse of London's foreign trade where the exports were largely cloth and the imports a mass of miscellaneous goods. The coasting trade supplied London mainly with fuel, food and metals. The fuel was chiefly coal from Newcastle, and it reached London in impressive quantities. Figures are available for only a few years, but they show 37,590 tons reaching London in 1585–6 and 54,742 tons in 1591–2.[126] There is no evidence that London exported any of this coal, though a few chaldrons were sometimes sent to south coast ports and a good deal may have gone up the Thames. The remainder was consumed in London, probably largely for domestic heating. Coal was supplemented by some firewood in the form of billets and faggots, which came chiefly from the Kentish and Sussex ports of Rochester, Milton, Faversham, Rye and Winchelsea.[127] Milton, for example, sent 35,000 billets and sixteen loads of unspecified size between Easter and Michaelmas 1580;[128] Rye exported very large amounts of billets as well as sending them to London, which did not prevent the town from complaining bitterly about the scarcity of wood and attributing it to the ironworks.[129]

London had to be fed as well as warmed. The basic foodstuffs of man and beast were not imported except in years of scarcity and so they had to be brought by land, river or the coasting trade.[130] Meat arrived on foot, if not yet from as far away as Scotland, perhaps from as far away as Wales. Grain had no such built-in locomotion; a good deal of it was brought to the capital by the coasting trade from the ports of the east and south-east coasts. The northern limit of supply seems to have been Hull, which sent wheat, rye, barley and malt.[131] Boston sent some malt, beans and barley,[132] but was quite overshadowed by King's Lynn, which was one of the great grain ports, drawing its supplies from Norfolk and from the arable farms of the interior tapped by the Ouse. The shipments of grain from King's Lynn could exceed ten thousand quarters in certain years, but the trade fluctuated widely and the annual average must have been much lower than that.[133]

Along the Norfolk coast Blakeney and Great Yarmouth were grain ports too with combined shipments to London that could reach six to seven thousand quarters in a good year.[134] There was a similar, though probably smaller, trade from Ipswich, Colchester and Maldon. In 1578 for example Maldon's trade was mainly with London and much of it was in wheat, oats and 'beer corn'.[135] Finally the Kentish ports were great shippers of grain to London: wheat and malt from Sandwich and Rochester, wheat, wheatmeal, oats and malt from Faversham, wheat, wheatmeal, oats, barley and malt from Milton.[136] These ports were comprised within the head ports of Sandwich and Deal and their members. Together these shipped 10,853 qrs of corn to London in 1561–2.[137] This grain trade was important, but it is impossible to say how much of the grain London consumed as food, drink and fodder was received by the coast. Gras estimated London's total consumption of corn in 1605 as 550,000 qrs. This was based on a population of 224,275 consuming $2\frac{1}{2}$ qrs per head per annum, together with an additional 50,000 qrs to cover 'ship's provision, horses, fodder and corn in beer exported'.[138] This is mere guesswork, but if it were anywhere near the truth, it would imply that quite a small proportion of the corn London consumed was obtained through the coasting trade. It would equally imply that a great deal of it was obtained by land, which was probably true.

Apart from corn, the main foodstuffs London obtained by the coasting trade were butter, cheese and fish. Though some butter came from Hull in the north and Chichester, Poole and Lyme Regis in the south,[139] the main source of supply for both butter and cheese was Norfolk, Suffolk and Essex. Both King's Lynn and Great Yarmouth sent some butter and cheese to London, but Suffolk was more important, sending 4,179 barrels of butter and 3,768 weys of cheese in 1585–6.[140] Most of the Suffolk ports were engaged in this trade, for shipments are recorded from Dunwich, Aldeburgh, Orford, Woodbridge and Ipswich. Camden observed that great store of cheese was made in Suffolk and 'vented into all parts of England'.[141] He also noted that in Essex the cheese was made from ewes' milk and that men took women's office by doing the milking. This cheese was sold in all parts of England and exported 'for the rusticall people, labourers and handicraftesmen to fill their bellies and feed upon'.[142] Whether this was the cheese that went to London is uncertain, but Colchester and Maldon sent both butter and cheese to the capital.[143] Fish were more varied in kind than butter and cheese. There were salmon from Berwick and Chester, pilchards from Looe, and pilchards, hake, ling and newland fish from Plymouth.[144] These were much less important than the cod and ling from King's Lynn, Blakeney and Faversham, and the herring from Great Yarmouth, Blakeney, Dunwich, Aldeburgh and Colchester.[145]

London's coastwise trade in metals seems to have embraced copper, lead, tin and iron. Copper from the Mines Royal at Keswick was shipped from Newcastle to London.[146] Newcastle also sent some lead (as did Hartlepool), but the main source of lead was Hull, where the north Yorkshire and Derbyshire lead converged.[147] Thus in 1600 Hull shipped 1,692 fodders of lead to London or 91 per cent of its coastwise shipments of lead.[148] Tin was a product of the south-west and was shipped to London from the Cornish ports of Truro, Helston, Helford and Fowey, often in ships which carried no other cargo. Some also went from Dartmouth, Plymouth and Exeter and even Poole which re-shipped some Cornish tin to London.[149] Finally, London got its iron from the Weald by way of the Sussex ports, Winchelsea, Hastings, Rye, Pevensey, Shoreham and Newhaven.[150]

Though fuel, food and metals cover the main categories of goods shipped to London by the coast, there were other goods of some importance. Nothing need be added to what has already been said about cloth shipments, except to repeat that they seem to have been surprisingly small. Some of the raw materials of the cloth industry were shipped to London, for example woad from Poole, Southampton, Lyme Regis and Exeter,[151] which were well placed for the import of Toulouse woad. Alum, too, was shipped from Southampton, Poole and Exeter.[152] Starch came from Sandwich where it may have been a local speciality for it was specifically described as 'Sandwich starch'.[153] Timber in all forms, barrel boards, ceiling boards, laths etc., came from Arundel.[154] There were calf-skins from Ipswich and lamb and coney skins from Boston.[155] In 1580 Faversham received raw hides from London and returned tanned hides to London.[156] Even so, the movement of skins, hides and leather seems small. All the goods sent to London had one thing in common: very few of them entered directly into the export trade, perhaps only some of the cloth, lead, tin and copper.

The goods sent out from London by the coasting trade had often formed part of London's imports. They sometimes give the impression that those great miscellaneous cargoes from Antwerp or Amsterdam had been divided up, put on board the coasting ships and despatched to the provincial ports. In a sense they had. This is interesting enough as an example of the movement of goods, but it does not make an analysis of that movement very easy. All that can be done is to suggest the main categories of goods and indicate their relative importance, taking the Port Book for 1585–6 as a basis.[157] The goods can be loosely grouped into the broad headings of food and drink, raw materials and manufactured goods.

The drink consisted of wine and beer. London shipped some wine, chiefly to the east and south coast ports, but it does not seem to have been an important trade. Many places imported their wine directly and had a coasting trade of their own in it. Beer is more surprising in view of the belief that it was essentially a local product which was difficult to transport without deterioration. In fact London shipped beer in considerable quantities; in 1585–6 it went to two dozen ports ranging round the coast from Berwick in the north to Helford in the south-west. There is no evidence that any cider was received or shipped out. The food was much more varied than the drink. It included dried fruit (raisins, currants and above all prunes for which the Elizabethans clearly had a passion); sugar and treacle, salt and vinegar. It no doubt included spices, but these, and probably other things, were concealed under the entry 'grocery wares'. Grocery wares in a bewildering variety of boxes, chests, hampers etc. were shipped to most of the provincial ports with which London traded. Most of these food stuffs had originally been imported; London was re-shipping them on their way to the provincial grocers.

The raw materials were re-shipments too, either of goods London had imported or of goods it had received by the coasting trade. Thus London shipped a good deal of iron to east coast ports, and especially to Hull, King's Lynn and Great Yarmouth;[158] this had either been imported or was the re-shipment of Wealden iron. Some iron went to south coast ports as far west as Truro; this was presumably imported iron for there was little point in shipping Wealden iron to London and then back along the south coast. Similarly a little of the tin from the south-west was re-shipped to east coast ports. The steel, which London shipped in small quantities to east and south coast ports, was almost certainly imported. The same was true of the pitch and tar which had a very wide circulation extending from the north-east ports right round to Liverpool. Hops had a similar circulation. Most of the remaining raw materials were connected with the cloth industry. They included a little wool, some of it Spanish, flax, alum and a great deal of oil, not all of which may have been destined for cloth making. They also included dyestuffs, of which woad and madder occur most frequently. Again many of these things had almost certainly been imported.

The manufactured goods shipped from London are more difficult to determine. A great many of them were simply described as haberdashers', ironmongers', upholsterers' and braziers' wares. The most common were haberdashers' wares, which may have included some clothes, though clothes are sometimes specified. In 1580 Milton received from London two hampers 'newe shooes' and a truss of 'made wares for maryners apparell',[159] in 1586 Great Yarmouth got frieze gowns and seven dozen 'dobletts and breeches',[160] and in 1595 Lyme Regis got '9 doz. petycotes',[161] which suggests that all clothes were not bespoke. Haberdashers' wares must have included some of those expensive imported cloths that are found in the stock of provincial drapers, mercers and haberdashers. London shipped some cloth that was specifically described. This included linen as well as the woollen cloth that was probably destined for export. Of other goods soap was very important; it went to most of the ports with which London traded. Stone pots, too, for some reason had a wide circulation; they were probably stone drinking pots from Germany.[162] It would be tedious to enumerate all the goods London shipped; they included glass and glasses, paper, pans and kettles, shovels and nails, cables and ropes and almost everything else.

It is fitting that London should appear as Emporium in Harrington's *Oceana*, for it received and distributed goods on a large scale, but it is easy to exaggerate its role in the coasting trade of the country as a whole. Some provincial ports were dominated by their London trade, but to many that trade was only a part of their coasting trade and not always the bigger part. This becomes clear when the coasting trade of the east coast ports is examined from the provincial rather than from the London angle. Newcastle

31

upon Tyne is rightly regarded as the great supplier of coal for the London market, but the whole picture is not as simple as that. Newcastle was a very odd town by Elizabethan standards. It was large, with a population of perhaps 10,000, and its economy rested on the mining and shipping of coal. It is curious that the 'backward' north should have contained in Newcastle perhaps the largest purely industrial town in the country and in the Mines Royal the biggest integrated mining and manufacturing concern in the country. Newcastle did not exist simply by supplying coal to London. Some coal was exported, though the quantity was not large, and a great deal of coal was shipped to the provincial ports of the east coast. Thus in 1591–2 Newcastle shipped coastwise 45,710 Newcastle chaldrons or 93,705 tons of coal of which 26,068 chaldrons or 54,742 tons went to London.[163] The remainder went to east coast ports with a little even going along the south coast. As a big industrial town Newcastle was dependent on 'imported' food. This did not come from London, apart from some beer and groceries, but largely from the bigger provincial ports to which the bulk of the coal was sent. It was from Hull and King's Lynn that Newcastle got most of the grain to feed its industrial population. Indeed it is possible that, in most years, the coasting trade between Newcastle and other provincial ports was greater in value than that between Newcastle and London.

The Newcastle trade meant that some of the east coast ports faced as it were both ways in their coasting trade, northwards to Newcastle and southwards to London. Thus Hull got large amounts of coal from Newcastle, some 8,874 tons in 1584–5,[164] and supplied Newcastle with barley, wheat, rye, malt and peas. Grain also went to Berwick, Hartlepool, Whitby and Scarborough. But it went southwards, too, to London as did lead, butter and cheese. In return London sent a mass of miscellaneous goods (groceries, haberdashery, dyestuffs etc.).[165] This was a fairly common pattern, but sometimes a strand was missing. Boston got its coal from Newcastle, some 1,845 tons between Easter and Michaelmas 1584, but its barley, beans and malt went southwards, largely to London in exchange for wine, iron, pitch and tar, soap and the usual grocers', haberdashers' and ironmongers' wares.[166] The full pattern was resumed at King's Lynn, a much greater port than Boston, whose ancient glories as a wool staple had departed. King's Lynn had an extensive and quite intricate coasting trade.[167] It got large amounts of coal from New-castle, almost twenty thousand tons in some years, and sent large amounts of grain, especially rye, to Newcastle. Grain also went to Berwick (especially malt for the garrison) and to Yorkshire ports. Southwards grain was shipped to London and other east coast ports. In the year of scarcity, 1586–7, it went as far as Bristol. In that year shipments to London exceeded shipments to Newcastle, but that was exceptional. Lynn's recorded shipments of grain to London never exceeded 30 per cent of its total grain shipments. In addition Lynn shipped fish and ropes and some butter and cheese to London. From London Lynn got iron (though some came direct from the Sussex ports), soap and a great mass of mis-cellaneous goods, some of which were re-shipped, not only up the Ouse but to other ports including Boston and Newcastle.

This pattern was repeated on a much smaller scale at Blakeney. In the half year Easter to Michaelmas 1587, Blakeney got 1,470 tons of coal and thirty 'stone winches' from Newcastle, timber from Arundel, some herrings from Blyth, a few cloths and oats from King's Lynn, and salt and miscellaneous goods from London and Great Yarmouth. In the same period Blakeney sent 28 qrs malt, 200 qrs rye, six combs of peas and two packs of dornix to Newcastle, grain to Manningtree, Ipswich and Boston, fish, malt (515 qrs), butter, candles, wax, saffron and a truss of feather beds to London, and miscellaneous goods, some of them imported, to King's Lynn and Great Yarmouth.[168] Further along the coast at Great Yarmouth, the link with Newcastle was weakening, for the trade was becoming more one-sided. Yarmouth got its coal from Newcastle (3,882 tons in 1580–1), but sent little in return. Yar-mouth's grain went largely to London and the ports of the south-east and south coast. London also took much of the fish and butter. In return London sent iron, soap, bay salt, beer, dyestuffs, groceries and a large range of varied goods. Some iron also came direct from the Sussex ports which also sent clapboard for the herring barrels. Some imported salt for the herrings came from the south coast ports too. Yarmouth's inward trade was strongly influenced by her position as the port of Norwich; much of the coal, groceries, soap and dyestuffs went up the Yare to warm, feed and employ the citizens of Norwich.[169]

Further south the ports of Suffolk and Essex felt the London pull more strongly, though they kept a link with Newcastle through the coal trade. Thus Dunwich and Aldeburgh sent their butter, cheese and fish to London, and Orford and Woodbridge their butter and cheese in return for the usual soap and groceries.[170] Ipswich got its coal from Newcastle and sent some wheat, malt, beans and butter in return, but much of its grain, butter and cheese went to London as did woad, fish and a little cloth in exchange for iron, soap, alum, dyestuffs, groceries etc.[171] Colchester showed much the same pattern of trade with coal from Newcastle and miscellaneous goods (groceries, soap, alum, dyestuffs, pitch and tar etc.) from London, but also some grain from Maldon, Boston and Blakeney and some fish from Ipswich. The outward trade was chiefly butter, cheese, grain and fish for London, grain, butter and cheese to Rochester, and fish to Faversham, Maldon and Hull.[172] Finally, Maldon's trade showed a similar though more one-sided pull of London. Maldon seems to have shipped little but peas, butter, cheese and grain, very largely to London. The inward shipments included coal and lead from Newcastle, grain from Ipswich 'usque Burnham' and miscellaneous goods from London.[173]

South of the Thames the provisioning of London continued from the Kentish ports. Thus Rochester sent wheat, timber and iron (including ordnance and shot) to London in return for miscellaneous goods which included a good deal of native cloth (kerseys, cottons, dozens). Some wheat went to east coast ports like Colchester and Aldeburgh and some rye as far as Newcastle, from which Rochester drew its coal. Some iron also went north to King's Lynn and Hull. Inward shipments, apart from those from London and Newcastle, seem to have been largely malt from Faversham, Margate and Sandwich.[194] Milton also got malt from these ports as well as butter and cheese from Maldon and Colchester, coal from Newcastle and Blyth and miscellaneous goods, again including native cloth, from London. But Milton's trade was really dominated by the shipment of wheat to London.[175] Faversham's trade was dominated in the same way; large quantities of wheat (and billets and tanned hides) to London, small quantities of wheat to Sussex and Essex ports. In return Faversham got miscellaneous goods (including raw hides and cloth) from London, butter and cheese from Suffolk and Essex, and a little coal from Newcastle.[176] Sandwich's trade had a similar pattern, but here malt was as important as wheat. Sandwich shipped wheat or malt not only to London but northwards to Berwick and Newcastle and westwards to Dartmouth, Plymouth and Penzance. In return came miscellaneous goods (including cloth) from London, coal from Newcastle, timber from Arundel and New Shoreham, iron from Rye and Pevensey, and salt from Dartmouth and Saltash.[177] There is no doubt that these Kentish ports had a complex pattern of trade that centred on, but was not monopolised by, London. They retained connections with other east coast ports through their trade in coal, butter and cheese, but such connections grew weaker in the south coast ports.

The trade of the Sussex ports reflected the economy of the Weald, which had little if any water communication with the coast and so distributed its products from a string of small ports stretching westward from Rye to Chichester. These ports shipped large quantities of iron to London and smaller quantities to Sandwich and King's Lynn and westwards to Southampton, Dartmouth and Plymouth. Some of them, especially Rye, Arundel, Pevensey and New Shoreham shipped timber in various forms to London and the south-west ports. Most of the Sussex ports got cargoes of miscellaneous goods, many of them imported, from London, but they also got similar cargoes, which included wine, from Southampton and Poole. Except for Chichester, they obtained a good deal of grain (wheat, malt, barley) by the coast, chiefly from the Kentish ports and from Chichester itself.[178] Indeed Chichester seems to have shipped little but grain and that largely to south coast ports. It received some cargoes of miscellaneous goods from both London and Southampton, some woad from Lyme Regis and even got a little coal from Newcastle.[179] Chichester had very little foreign trade to provide the basis of a coasting trade;[180] in that it was overshadowed by Southampton.

Southampton had a foreign trade that could contribute to its coasting trade, but the contribution was greater from the imports than from the exports. Of Southampton's imports, wine, woad, alum, salt, oil, paper and sugar were shipped coastwise to London and to south coast ports (which also took some timber). By the 1580s and 1590s privateering was bringing to Southampton large cargoes of sugar, much of which was re-shipped to London. Thus Southampton distributed imported goods by the coast as well as some native timber and beer, but the coasting trade made only a limited contribution to exports. The chief of these was cloth, which came almost wholly by land. Tin, which came from the Cornish ports, was an important export, but iron, which came from the Sussex ports and amounted to 311 tons in 1578–9, was not. Nor apparently was the fish from Great Yarmouth, Newhaven, Plymouth, Exeter and elsewhere. Though Southampton had an import trade of its own, that did not prevent it from getting miscellaneous cargoes from London, which included soap, stone pots, pitch and tar, hops, shovels and scoops, and from Poole, which included cider, paper, bottles and hops.[181]

Though little is known about Poole's foreign trade, it is clear that the port shipped both imported and native products by the coast. Thus Cornish tin, copperas, train oil, alum and some grain went to London in the 1560s, but by the 1580s and 1590s the trade consisted largely of English copperas, presumably from the copperas works on Brownsea Island. In the 1560s, too, tin, leather, woad, Seville oil and wine were going to Southampton, wine, alum and woad to Lyme Regis and woad, madder and honey to Topsham. Wine also went to Chichester, Rye and Shoreham, and bay salt to Newhaven and Hythe. In return Poole was getting miscellaneous goods from London and Southampton, tin from the Cornish ports and iron and timber from the Sussex ports. Between Michaelmas 1566 and Michaelmas 1567, forty-seven coasting vessels entered the port, of which twelve were from London, and fifty-one ships left, of which thirteen were for London,[182] but later evidence suggests a decline in the trade.[183]

In the same year, 1566–7, Poole's member port of Weymouth received fifteen coasters, of which two came from London. They brought miscellaneous goods (tar, soap, hops, madder, steel etc.) from London, woad, beer, wine and wood from Southampton, iron, hops, oil, prunes and oranges and lemons from Lyme Regis and iron from Newhaven. In the same twelve months eighteen ships left, of which two were for London. They carried largely malt, barley, wine and beer to south coast ports.[184] By the 1590s this trade was transformed by the shipment of prize cargoes of sugar to London. From Easter to Michaelmas 1595, Weymouth shipped 1,699 cwt sugar to London; in the single month of November 1601 prize sugar officially valued at £1,234 was landed at the port.[185] Poole's other member port, Lyme Regis, seems to have had a smaller share in the trade in prize goods. In the 1590s it was shipping some prize sugar to London as well as green woad, blockwood, sumach and cloth (dowlas and tregar from France). Dowlas also went to Lewes and Great Yarmouth, the latter taking woad and bay salt as well. Fowey and Plymouth took 'hogsheads in staves' presumably for the fishing industry. The inward shipments to Lyme Regis included wine, pilchards and Spanish iron from Plymouth, rye, bay salt and Spanish wool from Dartmouth, grain from New Shoreham and Great Yarmouth, and the usual miscellaneous goods from London.[186]

Exeter's coasting trade rather resembled Southampton's. There was the same absence of cloth, though cloth was Exeter's chief export; there was the same presence of tin, some brought from the Cornish ports for export. There was the same re-shipment of imported goods: alum to London, Bristol and Southampton, bay salt to Poole and Shoreham, wine to Plymouth and Poole, and Spanish iron to Lyme Regis and Poole. In return Exeter got coal from South Wales, woad and glass from Southampton, dried fruits from Plymouth, and the usual soap, groceries, pots and paper and other goods from London.[187] Exeter's member port of Dartmouth shipped some tin to London and salt to almost every port along the south coast. Its inward trade was more varied: tin from Cornwall, grain from Norfolk and Kent, timber from Arundel, malt, beer and copperas from Poole, some wine, pitch and tin from Southampton, and soap, dyestuffs, pitch and tar, hops and cordage from London.[188]

Plymouth was the last head port along the south coast, but for most of this period its coasting trade seems to have been small, especially in comparison with its considerable foreign trade. Though Plymouth had some trade with South Wales, from which it got cloth and coals, and with Bristol and the south coast ports, its main trade was with London. From London it got a bewildering variety of goods which included beer and hops, pitch and tar, cables and ropes as well as the usual soap, groceries and haberdashery. In return London took chiefly fish (pilchards, ling, hake, newland fish), train oil and bay salt, and some iron and Cornish tin.[189] By the 1590s these goods were quite overshadowed by the great shipments of prize sugar to London. Between Easter and Michaelmas 1592 Plymouth shipped 1,689 cwt sugar to London, between Easter 1594 and Easter 1595, 9,323½ cwt, and between Easter and Michaelmas 1595 a further 1,621¼ cwt.[190] Shipments on this scale were more valuable than Plymouth's normal coasting trade, but they were a product of war and therefore temporary. The Cornish ports, which were administratively under Plymouth, do not seem to have shared in this sugar trade. Their coasting trade was small. Fowey, Truro, Helston, and Helford all shipped tin, much of it for London. Looe sent fish to the capital. Fowey, Truro and Looe had some local trade, but all of them got miscellaneous goods from London. These included beer, soap, groceries, haberdashery wares, iron and hops. Presumably such goods provided return cargoes for the ships taking tin.[191] The north Devon ports and Bridgwater had some coasting trade. Barnstaple seems to have been the most important of them; it got an occasional cargo from London and traded with the South Wales ports and Bristol.[192] Indeed all these ports came within Bristol's orbit.

According to Camden, Bristol was 'so populous and well inhabited withall, that next after London and Yorke, it may of all cities in England justly challenge the chiefe place'.[193] This shows a fine disregard for the claims of Norwich, but William Smith described Bristol, rather incoherently, as 'one of the greatest and famoust citties in England'.[194] It was certainly the metropolis of the West and a Mecca for the youth of the Severn valley. Bristol had a substantial foreign trade, especially with France, Spain and Ireland. It was well situated as a distributive centre, with easy access to the ports of South Wales and the south-west and with communication by water up the Severn valley to Shrewsbury. All these features are reflected in its coasting trade. The ports of Monmouthshire and South Wales supplied Bristol with wool, cloth (frieze and cottons), mats, leather and skins (calf, lamb, sheep and goat). In return they received a mass of miscellaneous goods which included wine, iron, soap, alum, teazels and dyestuffs, dried fruits, drywares, and mercery, haberdashery and grocery wares. Much of this was a distribution by the coast of imported goods, and it is very reminiscent of the London trade in such goods. Bristol sent similar goods up the Severn and to the south-western ports, especially Bridgwater and Barnstaple, from which it received woad and iron, oil and wine. Most of this seems to have been short-distance trade, though occasionally it extended to Caernarvon and Beaumaris and to the south coast ports. There is little evidence of trade with London, and certainly Bristol does not appear to have received those miscellaneous cargoes from London that are such a feature elsewhere.[195] Fuller investigation might reveal them and a great deal more of interest about Bristol's trade.

Though Bristol dominated the coasting trade of the South Wales ports, it did not monopolize it. Those ports, from Cardiff to Haverfordwest, sent their wool and cloth to the south-western ports, and especially Barnstaple, from which they got wine, iron, linen, soap and other goods, apparently using Barnstaple as a miniature Bristol. Similar goods, in smaller quantities, were sent from Ilfracombe to Carmarthen and Tenby. Tenby also took iron, wine and canvas from Poole, wine and figs from Southampton and salt from Plymouth. There is little evidence of local trade between the South Wales ports, or between the south and central and North Wales. The coasting trade of North Wales centred on Beaumaris and Chester and not on the ports of the south.[196]

Chester acted as a distributive centre for goods to North Wales rather as Bristol did for South Wales, though Chester's trade was on a much smaller scale. Thus Chester sent cargoes of miscellaneous goods to Beaumaris and to a lesser extent to Caernarvon. They included canvas, linen, iron, wine, soap, dyestuffs, alum, hops and frying pans. They resemble Bristol's cargoes to the South Wales ports. On occasion Chester sent similar goods to Liverpool. Except in years of bad harvests, Chester supplied a good deal of grain by the coast; in 1594, for example, it was going to Ravenglass, Milnthorpe, Workington, Lancaster and Pwllheli. In return Chester received tanned hides and calf-skins from Beaumaris, wool from Ravenglass and wool and woolfells from Liverpool. But these were less interesting than the cargoes of miscellaneous goods from London, which included wine, iron, fuller's earth and chalk as well as the usual soap, dyestuffs, alum, hops and frying pans. The arrival of the London ship must have been like the arrival of 'the great ship from Amacon'. There is little evidence of return cargoes to London, though some salmon was sent in 1586. Presumably goods for London usually went by land, for the distance by land was only a quarter of that by sea. Though Chester had some trade with Liverpool, from which it got imported Irish goods, Liverpool itself received the occasional varied cargo from London, and shipped the occasional cargo of coal and grain to Beaumaris.[197] Further north the coasting trade was probably as scanty as the evidence for it.

It is obvious that the coasting trade was important in the movement of goods, but it is more obvious for some goods than for
others. The long-distance movement of coal, metals, corn, wine,
fuller's earth and timber would not have been economically possible by land, but many of the goods that entered into the coasting
trade, groceries, dyestuffs, haberdashery, for example, could have
stood the cost of even long-distance land carriage. Indeed they
must have borne that cost when destined for places remote from
any water carriage. If it paid to bring such goods as near as possible to their market by sea, even when the sea route was longer
than the land route, that must have been because of the relative
cheapness of sea transport. That cheapness was even more vital in
the long distance transport of bulky goods of low value. Yet very
little is known about the cost of carriage along the coast. Two
tombs for the third and fourth Earls of Rutland were carried by
sea from London to Boston in 1591 for £12 5s,[198] but that was a
rather special cargo, and it would be more interesting to know
what it cost to get a ton of coal from Newcastle to London. On the
analogy of the copper shipped from Newcastle to London, coal
should have cost about 7s to 8s a ton in freight. This was three or
four times the pit-head price, but carriage by land might have cost
anything from £5 a ton. Along the south coast there was traffic
between an iron works in Glamorgan and a steel works at
Robertsbridge in Sussex belonging to Sir Henry Sidney and his
partners. In 1565 21 tons of steel plates were shipped from Cardiff
to Rye at a cost in carriage of £33. Three years later the cost was
estimated at £1 a ton compared with 3s 4d a ton in land carriage
from the furnace to Cardiff.[199] Such random examples have little
value except to strengthen the view that carriage by sea was the
cheapest of all forms of carriage and was essential for some goods
going long distances.

Much of the long-distance transport by the coast was of goods
going to or coming from London. This made some contribution to
London as a centre of consumption, conspicuous or discreet.
Newcastle coal may have made more bearable that developing
London season which covered the winter months,[200] but the country gentlemen and their wives, who helped to make that season,
could satisfy their demand for exotic food, drink and cloth from
the cargoes coming directly to the capital from the Continent. The

contribution of the coasting trade, whether long distance or short, to London as a centre of production is more difficult to assess. The inward cargoes of tin and lead were essential to the London pewterers, and no doubt the iron was important to the smiths, the timber to the carpenters and joiners, and the woad and copperas to the dyers. It might be argued that the contribution of the coasting trade to London as a centre of production rested rather with the outward cargoes, which distributed the products of London industry to the provincial markets. There may be some truth in this in the case, for example, of soap and of those goods vaguely described as ironmongery, haberdashery and mercery wares, but it is more likely that most, but not all, of the manufactured goods shipped from London had been imported. The resemblance between the cargoes of miscellaneous goods imported from the continent[201] and the cargoes of miscellaneous goods shipped along the coasts is too close to be a mere coincidence. This would imply that London was essentially a distributive centre for imported goods. Given the concentration of foreign trade on London, such a role would make sense. Nor would such a role diminish the importance of London as a supplier of goods to provincial ports. It is a striking fact that almost every port of any size or importance had some trade with London, and that the trade included receiving large cargoes of miscellaneous goods. In such trade at least there seems to have been something of a national market. Indeed the movement of goods as a whole, by land, river and sea, suggests that a national market was emerging and was breaking down the frontiers of regional economies.

Notes
[1] T. Birch, *The history of the Royal Society*, iii. 208.
[2] Sir Herbert George Fordham, 'The earliest tables of the highways of England and Wales, 1541–61', *Trans. Bibliographical Soc.*, 2nd ser., viii (1927–8), 349–54; G. Scott Thomson, 'Roads in England and Wales in 1603', *English Historical Review*, xxxiii (1918), 234–43.
[3] William Smith, *The particular description of England 1588*, eds. H. B. Wheatley and E. W. Ashbee (London, 1879), pp. 46–7, 69–72.
[4] H. Robinson, *The English Post Office*, p. 15; J. A. J. Housden, 'Early posts in England', *English Historical Review*, xviii

(1903), 713–18.

[5] 2/3 Philip and Mary, c. 8.

[6] 5 Eliz. c. 13.

[7] T. Procter, *A worthy worke profitable to this whole kingdome, concerning the mending of all high-waies, 1607*; the 1610 edition has the title *A profitable worke to this whole kingdome*; W. T. Jackman, *The development of transportation in modern England*, (ed. 1962), p. 106.

[8] N. E. McClure, ed., *The letters of John Chamberlain*, ii. 408.

[9] *Shuttleworth accounts*, i. 54.

[10] *Ibid.*, i. 104.

[11] *Ibid.*, i. 74.

[12] *Ibid.*, i. 89.

[13] *Ibid.*, i. 10, 41.

[14] *Ibid.*, i. 53.

[15] *Ibid.*, i. 33.

[16] *Ibid.*, i. 38.

[17] *Ibid.*, i. 53.

[18] *Ibid.*, i. 59.

[19] *Ibid.*, i. 80.

[20] J. E. T. Rogers, *A history of agriculture and prices*, iv. 709–10; v. 770.

[21] *H. M. C. Cowper*, i. 130–1.

[22] Rogers, *op. cit.*, v. 769.

[23] W. G. Collingwood, *Elizabethan Keswick*, pp. 32, 66, 68.

[24] *Ibid.*, pp. 114, 122.

[25] *Ibid.*, pp. 52, 56.

[26] Sir William Beveridge, *Prices and wages in England*, i. 74–5.

[27] J. Humphreys, 'Elizabethan estate book of Grafton Manor', *Trans. Birmingham Arch. Soc.*, xliv (1920), 56.

[28] A. D. Dyer, *The city of Worcester in the sixteenth century*, p. 63.

[29] Rogers, *op. cit.*, v. 759, 775.

[30] W. G. Collingwood, *Elizabethan Keswick*, pp. 78–9.

[31] *Ibid.*, pp. 130–2, 183.

[32] B. C. Jones, 'Westmorland pack-horse men in Southampton', *Trans. Cumberland and Westmorland Antiquarian and Arch. Soc.*, n.s. lix (1960), 65–84.

[33] *H.M.C.* x. pt. iv. 317.

[34] Exch. K.R. Port Books, 1128/14.

[35] *Ibid.*, 1243/5.

[36] *Ibid.*, 641/11.

[37] R. Davis, *English overseas trade 1500–1700*, p. 53. This figure is 11 per cent higher than the one usually given because it includes the one cloth in ten allowed free as a wrapper.

[38] Exch. K.R. Port Books, 7/6.

[39] D. W. Jones, 'The "Hallage" receipts of the London cloth markets, 1562–*c*. 1720', *Economic History Review*, 2nd ser., xxv (1972), 567–87.

[40] Lansdowne MSS., 48, No. 45 (British Museum).

[41] *H.M.C.* xv. pt. x. 61.

[42] G. D. Ramsay, ed., *John Isham, mercer and merchant adventurer*, Northants Record Soc., xxi (1962), pp. xxvi, 73.

[43] T. S. Willan, ed., *A Tudor Book of Rates*, pp. xv–xvii.

[44] N. Lowe, *The Lancashire textile industry in the sixteenth century*, Chetham Soc., 3rd ser., xx (1972), ch. iv.

[45] H. J. Dyos and D. H. Aldcroft, *British transport*, pp. 42, 70.

[46] S. and B. Webb, *The story of the king's highway*, p. 64.

[47] W. G. Collingwood, *Elizabethan Keswick*, p. 32.

[48] *Shuttleworth accounts*, i. 129.

[49] J. U. Nef, *The rise of the British coal industry*, i. 381.

[50] J. Taylor, *The carriers cosmographie*, 1637 (Spenser Society, 2nd collection, 1873).

[51] *H.M.C.* xiv. pt. viii. 141.

[52] W. T. Jackman, *The development of transportation in modern England* (ed. 1962), p. 44.

[53] *Shuttleworth accounts*, i. 67.

[54] *H.M.C. Rutland*, i. 194.

[55] A. Raine, ed., *York civic records*, viii. 49–50, Yorks. Arch. Soc. Record Series, cxix (1953).

[56] D. M. Woodward, *The trade of Elizabethan Chester*, p. 69. The charge between London and Chester was said to be $\frac{3}{4}d$ or 'at the uttermost' 1d lb, which was about 9·2d to 12·3d a tonmile.

[57] Additional MSS., 34,218, ff. 37–40. (British Museum).

[58] D. M. Woodward, *The trade of Elizabethan Chester*, p. 70.

[59] T. C. Mendenhall, *The Shrewsbury drapers and the Welsh wool trade in the xvi and xvii centuries*, p. 35.

[60] For some examples see H. Thwaite, ed., *Abstracts of Abbotside wills 1552–1688*, Yorks. Arch. Soc. Record Series, cxxx (1968).

61 W. Smith, *The particular description of England*, pp. 4–5.

62 Harrison, 'Description', i. 78–168.

63 On York as a trading centre see D. M. Palliser, 'York under the Tudors: the trading life of the northern capital' in A. Everitt, ed., *Perspectives in English urban history*, pp. 39–59. On efforts to improve the river see B. F. Duckham, *The Yorkshire Ouse*, pp. 37–9.

64 M. Sellers, ed., *The York Mercers and Merchant Adventurers, 1356–1917*, Surtees Society, cxxix (1917), 167.

65 Exch. K.R. Port Books, 307/2, 19.

66 Sellers, *op. cit.*, pp. 168–9.

67 *Ibid.*, p. ii.

68 Harrison, 'Description', i. 159.

69 L. Stone, *Family and Fortune*, p. 194.

70 W. Smith, *The particular description of England*, p. 49.

71 W. Camden, *Britain* (ed. 1610), p. 712.

72 *H.M.C. Beverley*, p. 182.

73 Exch. K.R. Port Books, 306/17.

74 S. Revill, 'A 16th-century map of the River Trent near Shelford', *Trans. Thoroton Soc.*, lxxv (1971), 81–90; *Acts of the Privy Council, 1592–3*, pp. 440–1.

75 Camden, *op. cit.*, p. 547.

76 R. S. Smith, 'Huntingdon Beaumont. Adventurer in coal mines', *Renaissance and Modern Studies*, i (1957), 115–53; *H.M.C. Middleton*, pp. 171–83.

77 *Cal. State Papers Domestic, 1619–23*, p. 130, 532; *1629–31*, p. 548.

78 J. Harland, 'Early exports of Derbyshire lead', *The Reliquary*, vii (1866–7), 220–4.

79 Probably by the channel known as the By Carrs Dyke.

80 *H.M.C.* xiv. pt. viii. 65; J. W. F. Hill, *Tudor and Stuart Lincoln*, pp. 24–5, 84.

81 Harrison, 'Description', i. 170.

82 There is an excellent account of them, with useful maps, in Dorothy Summers, *The Great Ouse* (1973).

83 W. J. Jones, *The Elizabethan Court of Chancery*, p. 368, n. 3 for a case of 1563 between Cambridge and King's Lynn over landing rights at King's Lynn.

84 *H.M.C. Salisbury*, xv. 107.

85 V. Parker, *The making of King's Lynn*, p. 9.

44

[86] The best account of this river trade is in N. J. Williams, 'The maritime trade of the East Anglian ports, 1550–1590' (Oxford D.Phil. thesis, 1952), pp. 63–70. For trade on the Nen see also Fitzwilliam MSS., M277 (Northants Record Office).

[87] W. Haines, 'Stanford churchwardens' Accounts (1552–1662)', *The Antiquary*, xvii (1888), 172.

[88] W. H. Turner, ed., *Selections from the records of the city of Oxford, 1509–1583*, pp. 433–4.

[89] J. C. Jeaffreson, ed., *Middlesex county records*, i. 261.

[90] Harrison, 'Description', i. 82.

[91] W. Camden, *Britain* (ed. 1610), p. 389.

[92] J. E. T. Rogers, *A history of agriculture and prices*, v. 759, 775.

[93] Harrison, 'Description', i. 117.

[94] *H.M.C.* x. pt. iv. 444.

[95] C. A. J. Skeel, *The Council in the Marches of Wales*, p. 207.

[96] Exch. K.R. Port Books, 1128/13, 14.

[97] A. D. Dyer, *The city of Worcester in the sixteenth century*, pp. 61–2.

[98] Exch. K.R. Port Books, 1243/5.

[99] W. Hudson and J. C. Tingey, eds., *The records of the city of Norwich*, i. 223–4.

[100] N. J. Williams, 'The maritime trade of the East Anglian ports', pp. 72–7.

[101] W. Weston, *The autobiography of an Elizabethan*, trans. P. Caraman, pp. 1–3, 7–8.

[102] C. W. Chalklin, 'Navigation schemes on the upper Medway 1600–1665', *Journal of Transport History*, v (1961), 105–15.

[103] *H.M.C. Lord de L'Isle and Dudley*, i. 314–16.

[104] P. A. L. Vine, *London's lost route to the sea* (ed. 1965), pp. 20–2.

[105] *Supra*, p. 7.

[106] M. Sellers, ed., *The York Mercers and Merchant Adventurers, 1356–1917*, Surtees Society, cxxix (1917), 169–70.

[107] *H.M.C. Middleton*, p. 172.

[108] Westmorland MSS., (A) 4 xiii 9 (Northants Record Office).

[109] *H.M.C.* x. pt. iv. 443–4.

[110] 9 Henry vi. c. 5; 19 Henry vii. c. 18; 23 Henry viii. c. 12.

[111] C. W. Chalklin, 'Navigation schemes on the upper Medway 1600–1665', *Journal of Transport History*, v (1961), 105–15.

[112] 13 Eliz. No. 26 Private Act (House of Lords Record Office).

[113] 13 Eliz. c. 18.

[114] E. M. Hunt, *The history of Ware*, p. 18. For an interesting list of barges on the Lea see *H.M.C. Salisbury*, iii. 354–5.

[115] W. B. Stephens, 'The Exeter lighter canal, 1566–1698', *Journal of Transport History*, iii (1957), 1–11.

[116] *Acts of the Privy Council 1591–92*, p. 535.

[117] 1 Eliz. c. 15.

[118] G. Farr, 'Severn navigation and the trow', *Mariner's Mirror*, xxxii (1946), 66–95.

[119] M. K. James, *Studies in the medieval wine trade*, ed. E. M. Veale, pp. 139, 147.

[120] A. L. Simon, *The history of the wine trade in England*, iii. 38–9.

[121] James, *op. cit.*, p. 147.

[122] *Shuttleworth accounts*, i. 18, 45, 65, 74, 106.

[123] J. Humphreys, 'Elizabethan estate book of Grafton Manor', *Trans. Birmingham Arch. Soc.*, xliv (1920), 58.

[124] J. Webb, *Great Tooley of Ipswich*, pp. 93–115. This is a rare and excellent account of a merchant's inland trade.

[125] Harrison, 'Description' i. 182 lists fifty-five ports, havens and landing places in Essex alone. For an even longer list see E. P. Dickin, 'Notes on the coast, shipping, and sea-borne trade of Essex from 1565 to 1577', *Trans. Essex Arch. Soc.*, xvii (1924), 153–64.

[126] J. U. Nef, *The rise of the British coal industry*, ii. 381 gives 23,867 and 34,757 tons respectively, but Nef wrongly thought these coals were measured in London chaldrons of 26–27 cwt, whereas they were measured in Newcastle chaldrons of about 42 cwt. I have adjusted his figures accordingly. On coal measurements see T. S. Willan, *The English coasting trade 1600–1750*, pp. 208–9 and R. A. Mott, 'The London and Newcastle chaldrons for measuring coal', *Archaeologia Aeliana*, 4th ser., xl (1962), 227–39.

[127] Exch. K.R. Port Books, 7/6, 641/10, 12, 13.

[128] *Ibid.*, 641/10.

[129] *Ibid.*, 747/4; from May to Michaelmas 1592 Rye exported 332,000 billets; *H.M.C.* xiii. pt. iv. 75–6.

[130] On London's food supply see F. J. Fisher, 'The development of the London food market, 1540–1640' in *Essays in economic history*, ed. E. M. Carus-Wilson, i. 135–51 and N. S. B. Gras,

[131] Exch. K.R. Port Books, 7/6, 306/17, 307/2.

[132] *Ibid.*, 7/6, 390/4.

[133] Gras, *op. cit.*, pp. 306–7. Gras heads the table 'Lynn and members', but Lynn had no member ports.

[134] N. J. Williams, 'The maritime trade of the East Anglian ports', pp. 185–7.

[135] Exch. K.R. Port Books, 7/6, 591/5, 592/4, 7.

[136] *Ibid.*, 7/6, 641/10–13.

[137] *Gras, op. cit.*, p. 311.

[138] *Ibid.*, p. 77.

[139] Exch. K.R. Port Books, 7/6, 306/17, 864/7, 866/19.

[140] Williams, *op. cit.*, pp. 188–91; Exch. K.R. Port Books, 7/6, 592/7.

[141] W. Camden, *Britain* (ed. 1610), p. 459.

[142] *Ibid.*, pp. 441, 443.

[143] Exch. K.R. Port Books, 7/6, 591/15, 592/4.

[144] *Ibid.*, 7/6, 1014/18.

[145] *Ibid.*, 7/6, 591/15; Williams, *op. cit.*, pp. 192–8.

[146] W. G. Collingwood, *Elizabethan Keswick*, pp. 130–2.

[147] Exch. K.R. Port Books, 7/6, 306/17, 307/2.

[148] B. Hall, 'The trade of Newcastle-upon-Tyne and the North-East coast 1600–1640' (London Ph.D. thesis, 1933), p. 158.

[149] Exch. K.R. Port Books, 7/6, 864/7, 930/9, 1014/18.

[150] *Ibid.*, 7/7, 750/9, 10, 27. Newhaven often appears in the Port Books under its old name of Meeching.

[151] *Ibid.*, 7/6, 816/7, 866/19, 930/18.

[152] *Ibid.*, 7/6, 816/7, 864/7, 930/18.

[153] *Ibid.*, 7/6.

[154] *Ibid.*

[155] *Ibid.*, 7/6, 592/7.

[156] *Ibid.*, 641/13.

[157] *Ibid.*, 7/6.

[158] Hull got 113 tons of iron between Easter and Michaelmas 1574 (Exch. K.R. Port Books, 306/17); Williams, *op. cit.*, pp. 199–200.

[159] Exch. K.R. Port Books, 641/10.

[160] *Ibid.*, 7/6.

[161] *Ibid.*, 866/19.

[162] T. Wright, *Queen Elizabeth and her times*, ii. 124–5.

[163] J. U. Nef, *The rise of the British coal industry*, ii. app. D., tables (i) (*a*) and (iv), pp. 380–1.

[164] *Ibid.*, ii. 383.

[165] Exch. K.R. Port Books, 7/6, 306/17, 307/2. On the role of London merchants in this trade with Hull, see R. G. Lang, 'London's aldermen in business, 1600–1625', *Guildhall Miscellany*, iii (1971), 242–64.

[166] Exch. K.R. Port Books, 390/4.

[167] The best account is N. J. Williams, 'The maritime trade of the East Anglian ports', pp. 159–210, from which I have drawn most of my information.

[168] B. Cozens-Hardy, 'The maritime trade of the port of Blakeney, Norfolk, 1587–1590', *Norfolk Record Soc.*, viii (1936), 17–37.

[169] Williams, *op. cit.*, pp. 166–70, 184–6, 197–8.

[170] Exch. K.R. Port Books, 7/6.

[171] *Ibid.*, 592/7.

[172] *Ibid.*, 591/15.

[173] *Ibid.*, 592/4.

[174] *Ibid.*, 614/12; from Easter to Michaelmas 1580 Rochester got 474 tons of coal from Newcastle.

[175] *Ibid.*, 641/10; from Easter to Michaelmas 1580 111 ships entered or left Milton by the coast of which ninety-four were from or to London.

[176] *Ibid.*, 641/13.

[177] *Ibid.*, 641/11; from Easter to Michaelmas 1580 Sandwich got 1,055 tons of coal from Newcastle.

[178] *Ibid.*, 7/6, 641/11, 13, 816/7, 864/7, 930–9. There is much information on Rye's coasting trade in R. F. Dell, ed., *Rye shipping records, 1566–1590*, Sussex Record Soc., lxiv (1965–66); the shipments of 'lupins' (pp. 142–3 etc.) were presumably of hops.

[179] Exch. K.R. Port Books, 7/6, 739/24.

[180] *Ibid.*, 737/12, 738/21, 750/3.

[181] *Ibid.*, 7/6, 816/7, 8, 11. The best account of Southampton's trade is J. L. Wiggs, 'The seaborne trade of Southampton in the second half of the sixteenth century' (Southampton M.A. thesis, 1955). I have drawn a little information, including the iron shipments, from this thesis.

[182] Exch. K.R. Port Books, 864/7.

[183] *Ibid.*, 866/3, 13, 867/16, 17.

[184] *Ibid.*, 864/6.

[185] *Ibid.*, 866/17, 868/3.

[186] *Ibid.*, 866/19, 867/4.

[187] *Ibid.*, 930/18; W. B. Stephens, *Seventeenth-century Exeter*, p. 36.

[188] Exch. K.R. Port Books, 930/9.

[189] *Ibid.*, 1012/19, 1014/18, 1016/15.

[190] *Ibid.*, 1017/14, 1019/16, 17, 1019/19.

[191] *Ibid.*, 7/6, 1010/23, 1013/21, 1014/3.

[192] *Ibid.*, 7/6, 1083/14, 1128/13.

[193] W. Camden, *Britain* (ed. 1610), p. 237.

[194] W. Smith, *The particular description of England*, p. 34.

[195] Exch. K.R. Port Books, 1128/13, 14, 1243/5.

[196] For the Welsh coasting trade see E. A. Lewis, ed., *Welsh Port Books, 1550–1603*.

[197] Exch. K.R. Port Books, 1327/3. For Chester's coasting trade see also E. A. Lewis, *op. cit.* and D. M. Woodward, *The trade of Elizabethan Chester*, pp. 66–9.

[198] *H.M.C. Rutland*, iv. 398.

[199] *H.M.C. Lord de L'Isle and Dudley*, i. 316, 320.

[200] F. J. Fisher, 'The development of London as a centre of conspicuous consumption in the sixteenth and seventeenth centuries' in *Essays in economic history*, ed. E. M. Carus-Wilson, ii. 197–207.

[201] For examples see B. Dietz, ed., *The port and trade of early Elizabethan London*, London Record Society, viii (1972).

II THE PROVINCIAL RETAIL TRADE
IN ELIZABETHAN ENGLAND

The movement of goods was one aspect of the foreign and internal trade of the country. Much more is known of the foreign than of the internal trade, largely because the former was taxed through customs duties and therefore some record of it was kept. Such records provide statistical evidence of the volume and value of foreign trade which is largely lacking for internal trade. Of the two branches of internal trade, the wholesale and the retail, more is known about the wholesale than the retail as there have been studies of the wholesale trade in corn, wool and coal.[1] Though it is convenient to study these types of trade separately, from the point of view of the men engaged in them the distinction may sometimes be artificial. Merchants who engaged in foreign trade would normally be wholesalers and might be retailers even in London, where specilisation of function had gone further than in the provinces. This was the practical position, though contemporaries, with their belief in a well-ordered world of status, claimed to see and sought to maintain distinctions within the trading community, and especially the distinction between the merchant and the retailer. When William Harrison asserted that merchants 'often change estate with gentlemen, as gentlemen doo with them', he was thinking of merchants in foreign trade.[2] So too was the Lawyer in Wilson's *A discourse upon usury* when he wrote that 'the merchant adventurer is and maye be taken for a lordes fellow in dignitie, as well for hys hardye adventurynge upon the seas, to carrye our plentye, as for his royall and noble whole sales that he makes to dyvers men upon hys retourne, when he bryngeth in our want'. Here at least the obvious combination of foreign and wholesale trade was recognised, but to the Lawyer retailers were 'not worthy the name of merchaunts, but of hucksters, or chapmen of choyse, who, retayling small wares, are not able to better their own estate but wyth falsehode, lying and perjurye'.[3] This was an extreme view, but it was echoed by Philip Stubbes who included the tricks of tradesmen among his 'display of corruptions'.[4]

All this might be dismissed as the prejudice of moralists obsessed with 'degree', but in fact it had some practical importance when the monopolistic trading companies sought to apply such distinctions to their membership. Thus the Merchant Adventurers Company tried to limit its membership to 'mere merchants' and so exclude the retailer (and the craftsman). This attempt demanded some definition of retailer, and this was based not so much on the idea of direct sales to the consumer as on the quantity of the commodity sold, though there was of course an obvious connection between the two approaches. The Merchant Adventurers Company decreed that no member should 'keepe any open shoppe or shewe howse of his wares' and should not 'sell by lesse portion or quantity' than the Company stipulated. An elaborate schedule under seventy-three headings laid down the minimum quantities a member could sell without being classed as a retailer and so forfeiting his membership. The minimum quantity of many imported cloths was the piece; of currants, prunes and dates, wax and flax, battery and ironmongery it was the hundredweight, and of small haberdashery wares the gross. These were clearly wholesale quantities, and if enforced would have excluded the retailer, but they applied only to members 'resident in London or in the suburbes'. Provincial members of the Company successfully challenged the ruling that they should not be retailers, and in Hull, York, Newcastle and elsewhere it was possible to be a retailer and a member of the Merchant Adventurers Company. Even then it was stipulated that provincial members should not sell by less than the yard or the pound.[5] To sell less than these amounts was presumably the role of the pedlar or chapman.

Other trading companies adopted the same restrictive attitude. The Spanish Company of 1605 confined its membership to mere merchants and, in order to avoid 'all ambiguities and questions which may arise or growe upon the definition of a retailor', proceeded to define a retailer. Anyone was a retailer who sold any merchandise 'commonly sould by the hundreth, by any lesse waight than the hundreth, or any marchaundizes commonly sould by the pounde, by any lesse waight then the dozen pounde', though cloves, mace, cinnamon and nutmeg could be sold by the half dozen pounds. Similarly a retailer was one who sold 'any kinde of cloth . . . by lesse measure then the peece or half peece'.[6] In theory these restrictions applied to provincial as well as London merchants. This method of defining a retailer was used by the state in its economic legislation. An Act of 1550 'for buyinge and sellinge of butter and cheese' declared that none should buy butter and cheese to sell again except by retail, and retail was defined as 'where a waye of cheese or barrell of butter' or less was sold at one time to one person in open shop, fair or market.[7]

These definitions and distinctions reveal something of what contemporaries thought retailing to be, but they do not reveal much about the mechanics of the retail trade. The problem can be simply stated. Once we get away from any idea of a Robinson Crusoe economy of self-sufficient communities and self-contained households, how in fact did the consumer obtain the goods that he did not himself produce? If it is thought that the consumer produced all that he consumed, then there is no problem, except perhaps the problem of ignorance. Obviously there were many possible sources of supply, and they can be considered under the headings of fairs and markets, pedlars, craftsmen and shops.

Fairs and markets have traditionally been studied from a legal rather than from an economic standpoint. This is largely because economic history developed late as a separate discipline and in so doing took over much of the approach of earlier constitutional historians with their emphasis on legal origins and institutional frameworks. That approach is now giving way to a more economic one, especially as the agrarian historians emerge from their ivory shippons. This is very noticeable in the recent work on fairs and markets[8] which, in the present state of knowledge, leaves little to be said. It is clear that fairs were centres of both wholesale and retail trade. The Londoners who sent their groceries to the Cross Fair at Beverley were providing a source of supply for Yorkshire grocers. The farmers or dealers who brought their cattle and sheep to the fairs at Worcester were providing meat for the city's butchers.[9] The retail trade of the fairs has left some trace in the household accounts of gentry families. Thus the Shuttleworths of Smithills and Gawthorpe and the Talbots of Grafton Manor bought fish at Stourbridge Fair, as did Roger Lord North of Kirtling.[10] But North, who also bought fish at Ely Fair, bought much else at Stourbridge. In 1577 his purchases included salt, soap, currants, raisins, prunes, sugar, baskets and pails, two kettles and a frying pan and gunpowder and matches. In the 1550s Sir William Petre was getting salt fish from Stourbridge Fair, and hardware for the kitchen, cloths for the dairy house, nails and other goods at Ingatestone and Chelmsford Fairs.[11] These examples may be a biased sample of well-to-do purchasers who kept accounts, but it is possible that most retail buying at fairs was done by such people, who bought in fairly large quantities for large households. Though many places had more than one fair in the year, fairs could only provide a very intermittent source of supply, which was not suitable for the consumer who wished to buy in small and regular quantities. Such a consumer was likely to find the weekly market more useful.

There were some eight hundred market towns in England and Wales, but their distribution was uneven. They were thin on the ground in Wales and the north of England (except for Lancashire) where a visit to market could involve a journey of twenty miles or more. Elsewhere the density of market towns was greater and so the journeys shorter.[12] Wherever they were, markets were centres of exchange between town and country. There seems no doubt that they provided the ordinary consumer with his main source of those native foodstuffs he did not himself produce. This would be difficult to prove, for those families which kept household accounts were just the ones most likely to get such foodstuffs from their home farms or direct from their tenants. There is little clear evidence in the Shuttleworth accounts of buying in markets though it almost certainly occurred. It is perhaps significant that such things as butter, cheese, eggs and bacon do not figure in the probate inventories of shopkeepers. It might be argued that such goods were perishable and so were disposed of before the inventory was made, but in fact such inventories were nearly always made immediately after the death of the shopkeeper. The more reasonable explanation is that such things were usually bought in the market, and in that sense the market and the shop were complementary rather than competitive. Nor should it be forgotten that country folk came to market to buy as well as to sell. Market day was the shopping day. Though markets were very important, the range of goods they offered was largely limited to the natural products of their hinterland. Those who wanted more varied goods had to look elsewhere.

It is widely believed that such customers looked to the pedlar

53

for their supplies, but there is little clear evidence to support this belief. The activities of pedlars have left little trace in this period. An Act of 1552 declared that 'tynkers, pedlers and suche like vagrant persones are more hurtfull then necessarie to the commen wealth of this realme', and no person or persons 'commenly called pedler, tynker or pety chapman shall wander or go from one towne to another or from place to place out of the towne, parishe or village where such person shall dwell, and sell pynnes, poyntes, laces, gloves, knyves, glasses, tapes or any suche kynde of wares whatsoever, or gather connye skynnes' unless they were licensed by two justices of the peace. The licence was to assign a 'circuyte or compasse' in which the holder could operate.[13] There is little evidence that such licensing was carried out; it does not seem to have been recorded in the minutes of quarter sessions as was the grant of licences to badgers of corn. There is, however, some evidence of continued hostility to pedlars. An undated Elizabethan document accused them of being for the most part 'vacabonds and wanderers in all partes', whose activities led to the decay of trades in cities and towns where tradesmen were 'spoyled and ympoverished' and poor people were reduced to begging for want of work. Pedlars were also accused of spoiling markets and fairs 'by unorderlie exposinge comodities to sale' and of committing murders and robberies whereby sin and wickedness were increased. The remedy was to suppress pedlars by selling their goods to the Queen's use and fining them 40s, of which half was to go to the informer and half to be used to maintain the poor and houses of correction.[14] Too much should not be made of these familiar tirades, but this one raises a point of interest. It bears the marks of an urban protest against unauthorised trading within towns at a time when official municipal policy aimed at confining retail trade to freemen except during fairs and markets. It therefore raises the question of how far pedlars were free to trade within towns. No doubt they could trade on market days like anyone else. At Manchester in 1560 pedlars, butchers and others were ordered to make clean their stalls or standings in the market or pay 1d a quarter to the market cleaners.[15] At other times and places it may have been more difficult for the pedlar. On 17 December 1573 the Merchant Adventurers Company of Newcastle decreed that no member should buy any manner of wares from Richard Natteres of Gateshead, chapman, Thomas Gilbert, pedlar, 'presentlie dwelling within this towne', or from any other chapman or pedlar dwelling in Gateshead or Newcastle. The reason for this ban was that such chapmen and pedlars were 'not free with us of this Feoloship'. It was a curious case; Natteres had a shop in Gateshead, and a month earlier Gilbert had been bound in £200 not to sell to any but members of the Company, an obligation which presumably he had not kept.[16] Whatever lay behind all this, it suggests a restrictive attitude towards the trading activities of pedlars in towns.

It is possible that pedlars should be regarded as supplying rural rather than urban customers. That seems to be the traditional picture of the pedlar going round the villages, farms and the big houses. It is probably the true picture, but it leaves little trace. The Shuttleworths record one purchase from a pedlar, of $3\frac{1}{4}$ oz of pepper at $4d$ oz in May 1601,[17] and later, in 1613, the Howards of Naworth Castle, a more remote residence, bought ribbon and pins 'at the gate'.[18] The problem is to discover not only who were the pedlar's customers but also who were his suppliers. The very scanty evidence on this suggests that the shopkeeper was one source of supply. In April 1581 William Wray, a Ripon mercer, sold to Thomas Marshall, a petty chapman of Potton in Bedfordshire, small quantities of pepper, saffron, onion seeds, linen cloth, lace and laces and points and incle. The sales were made on 13, 14, 20, 25 April, and they totalled £4 11s 3d. Some of the goods seem to have been sold to Marshall at less than the normal retail price.[19] It is not possible to be certain of this, but it would be a logical concession to someone who was himself going to re-sell. On another occasion Wray was paid £8 10s by 'John Wilson pedler for wares'.[20] A rather curious definition of the retailer in the Spanish Company's ordinances of 1605 also suggests the shopkeeper as a supplier of pedlars. It ran 'he that keepeth open shopp or warehowse in the streate, and usually selleth wares to chapmen by retaile, shalbe accoumpted a retailor'.[21] Fairs may have been another source of supply for pedlars. In 1568 David ap Jenn of Monmouthshire attended the St Dennis Fair at Hereford and bought sugar candy, pepper, thread, pins, girdles and knives. As he was unable to pay for a standing at the fair, he was going to take his purchases back into the country to sell.[22] He sounds like a pedlar, and it is interesting to note that he had intended both to buy goods and to sell them at the fair. Though little can be discovered about pedlars, they undoubtedly had a role in retail trade, but those who see them as the only alternative to the fair and the market seem to exaggerate that role.

The role of the craftsman in retail trade, on the other hand, seems to have been underestimated and rarely explored.[23] Clearly many craftsmen did not produce articles which they sold to the consumer, for example craftsmen in the building trades and in many branches of clothmaking. Other craftsmen did, however, produce such articles, and the interesting point is how far they worked to order and how far in anticipation of demand. Provincial tailors seem to have worked entirely to order using material supplied by their customers. They were paid for their work rather as weavers were paid for weaving yarn 'put out' to them. At death they left no stock, only the tools of their trade, which were usually shears, a pressing iron and the board on which they sat at work. It was quite different with shoemakers, saddlers, pewterers and goldsmiths. They usually had a stock which they retailed. Thus Thomas Mayho, a shoemaker of Banbury, had '16 dozen of shoes' and '2 paire of bootes' in stock when he died in 1571. They were valued at £11 3s 4d. Three years later Thomas Allins, another Banbury shoemaker, had twenty-seven dozen and one pair of shoes valued at 13s 4d a dozen, and two pairs of boots at 4s a pair.[24] A Devon shoemaker, Lawrence Wyndeat, had 'seaven dozen shoes great and small and one paire of bootes' valued at £4 11s 4d at his death in 1590. He was owed 7s 5d for shoes, which shows that he sometimes sold on credit.[25] Finally Robert Pavie, a Worcester shoemaker who died in 1594, left in his shop fourteen pairs of men's shoes valued at £1 12s, fourteen pairs of women's shoes valued at 14s, eight pairs of children's shoes valued at 4s and two pairs of boots valued at 8s.[26] These probate valuations seem low, but when a labourer broke into a Chelmsford shoemaker's shop in 1560 and got away with fifty-seven pairs of shoes, they were valued at only £2 13s 4d.[27] Moreover it should be remembered that shoes were less substantial then than they are today. When William Freke was an undergraduate at Oxford from 1619 to 1622, he bought nineteen pairs of shoes, three pairs of boots and a pair of pantofles. He was only fourteen when he went up to the university, so he was buying boys' shoes and boots. Though four pairs of the shoes cost only about 1s a pair, the usual price was 2s 4d to 2s 8d a pair; the boots cost 7s to 8s 6d a pair, which can be compared with the 7s to 8s for a pair of garters and the 6s 6d to 7s for a pair of stockings. Freke did not simply discard his shoes when they were worn; on nine occasions he paid 'for repairs to them'.[28] All this suggests that shoes were not very expensive in comparison with other items of clothing and that they were not very durable.

There is less information on the stocks held by other craftsmen, but it points in the same direction. Thus Elinor Pare, the widow of an Oxford saddler, had 'sadles and small wares and sadle trees and tooles' valued at £8 'in the shopp' at her death in 1583.[29] Ten years later George Rochester, a Newcastle saddler, had a selection of saddles, bridles, stirrup leathers and iron, and harness and girth buckles. His stock of leather and of saddle trees ready for covering implies that he was a working saddler.[30] Some leather workers may have sold wholesale rather than retail as many Chester glovers plainly did,[31] but Thomas Johnes, 'jirkin maker' of Gateshead, with his stock of pantofles, 'pompes', buskins and 'eight maid jerkins' was clearly a craftsman-retailer.[32] So too were some of the workers in metal with their stocks of consumer durables. Thus Henry Green, a pewterer and bell founder of Worcester, had pewter pots, salts and spoons, and brass kettles and pots in stock at his death in 1569.[33] Mathew Wilkinson, a smith of Newcastle who died in 1582, had a stock of three score and sixteen dozen 'showeles' as well as a variety of hammers and eight pairs of tongs.[34] The hammers and tongs may have been his work tools, though they seem a bit numerous for that. Perhaps he was a specialised shovel maker. Goldsmiths, too, had their stock of plate, part of which may have been unredeemed pledges. Robert Walshman, a Manchester goldsmith who died in 1598, had plate (salts, bowls, beaker and jug etc.) valued at £24 10s 10d, but he also had spoons, a salt and a goblet held in pawn 'whereon money is lente'.[35]

It would be tedious to enumerate all the types of craftsmen who were also retailers. Clearly such craftsmen must be considered as one form of shopkeeper, but they differ from other provincial shopkeepers in two respects. Firstly they sold goods they had themselves made or, more accurately, that had been made in their workshops, for doubtless many took apprentices and employed journeymen. Of the master shoemakers in Chester in 1599, eighteen employed a total of forty-four journeymen.[36] Secondly, because they sold goods they had made, their stock was limited in variety and therefore as retailers they were more specialised than other shopkeepers. The special features of the retail trade carried on by craftsmen do not mean that such trade was unimportant. The limited variety of the stock has to be balanced against the number of the outlets. When it is remembered how numerous craftsmen were in town and country, it would be wrong to under estimate their contribution as retailers.

Though the craftsman-retailer may be considered as a special sort of shopkeeper, the shopkeeper as normally understood differed in his activities from the other forms of retailing. His trade was not periodic like the fairs and markets; he was not peripatetic like the pedlar, and, unlike the craftsman, he sold goods which he had not produced. Perhaps the common factor in all this is simply our ignorance of retail trade, which extends to the shopkeeper. There is a history of shopping,[37] but not of shops. This neglect of shops and shopkeepers can hardly be a survival of the Victorian snobbery about trade and tradesman. Indeed there seem to be two main reasons for the neglect. The first is the belief that shops were not very important, especially in comparison with other forms of retailing. Thus Miss Deane considers that periodic fairs 'constituted the most important wholesale and retail outlet' in the mid eighteenth century. She concedes that 'the shop had begun to supplant the pedlar or the itinerant tradesman of the fairs before the end of the eighteenth century, but the fixed retail shops with window display and a wide range of goods . . . were still confined to the larger towns'.[38] Apart from the question of window display, which does not seem very relevant, this view under estimates the importance of shops before the eighteenth century. But if shops were so unimportant, why indeed study them?

The second reason for neglect is the difficulty of the subject, and it is a difficulty of sources. It is not known whether many Elizabethan shopkeepers kept records of their business, but certainly hardly any of such records have survived. The business records now drifting into the county record offices are largely of the nineteenth century, and it is doubtful whether many sixteenth-century ones will turn up. This means that shops and shopkeepers have to be studied obliquely from other sources which have a bearing on their activities. Something can be learned from the records of towns, especially from the occupations of those admitted to the freedom of the town.[39] More can sometimes be learned from the records of gilds, but gilds are now an unfashionable and neglected subject, and wrongly so. The records of the law courts, especially of Chancery and the Court of Requests, may contain information on retail trade as they do on wholesale trade, but their primitive calendars make them a time-consuming lucky dip with a strong trend towards diminishing returns. Finally there are the probate inventories, which record personal property held at the time of death. These have become a fashionable source for economic and social history because they provide information which it is difficult or impossible to obtain elsewhere. They are certainly a very valuable source for the study of shops and shopkeepers. Their limitations are obvious. They give a static picture at the time of death. They record only personal property and not real estate, which means that they can be very misleading as evidence of the total wealth of an individual or of an occupational group. Their merits are equally obvious. They usually give a detailed list of the stock in hand, itemising every piece of cloth and every pound of spice, which makes it possible to see whether a shop was specialised or not. As personal property could only be assessed if the balance of the debts owed by and owing to the deceased were determined, inventories record such debts. Debts owed by the deceased may reveal what goods he bought on credit and where he obtained them. Debts owing to the deceased may show that he was selling on credit, but in fact it is usually impossible to tell the nature of these debts, whether they were for goods sold or for money lent. Where the debts were clearly for goods sold and where the domicile of the debtor is given, it is possible to get some idea of a shopkeeper's trading area. Probate inventories are so numerous and so scattered that they lend themselves to local rather than to national studies. More inventories of retail traders need to be published, but equally important is the need for more studies in depth of the retail trade of individual towns.

None of the sources available for the study of shops and shopkeepers in this period gives any detailed picture of the distribution of shops throughout the country. That the larger towns possessed shops is obvious. In 1555 Chester had at least seventeen drapers, nine mercers, eighteen butchers and six ironmongers;[40] in 1569 Norwich had 150 grocers, forty-eight mercers and twenty-nine butchers.[41] Even if the figures include wholesalers as well as retailers, as apparently they do at Norwich, they are still impressive evidence of the number of urban shops. Indeed the modern study of towns and their occupational structures has only served to emphasise the importance of the distributive trades. The real difficulty is to trace the existence of shops in small places, for on this the evidence is scanty and scattered. There are sources which show the existence of shopkeepers in places both large and small. Thus some provincial shopkeepers sent their sons to London to be apprenticed to members of the London Livery Companies, and their admission as apprentice was recorded together with their father's occupation and domicile. In this period the London Stationers Company recorded the admission of apprentices whose fathers were mercers in Haslewood, Yorkshire, (? Hasle near Pontefract), Bury St Edmunds, Braintree, Seal (Kent), Reading, Cardiff, Northampton, Hempstead, Coventry and Stafford. Other apprentices were the sons of haberdashers in Aylesbury, Wisbech, Derby and York, of grocers in Hempstead and Preston, and of booksellers in Lichfield, Astbury (Cheshire) and Audley (Staffordshire).[42] A mercer of Dronfield (Derbyshire) and one of Greystoke (Cumberland), a haberdasher of Woburn and a grocer of Hallaton (Leicestershire) each sent a son to be apprenticed to a member of the London Carpenters Company.[43] Similarly the scanty quarter sessions records supply some evidence on the distribution of shopkeepers. The Lancashire quarter sessions records for 1590 to 1603 show haberdashers at Wrightington, Harleton and Burscough, mercers at Clitheroe and Ormskirk, drapers at Bradford (near Manchester), Stretford, Ashley, Ormskirk, Cheetham and Stockport, butchers at Pendleton and Ribchester, shoemakers at Eccles, Eskrigg, Brindle, Westhoughton, Ribchester, Middleton and Pleasington, and a goldsmith at Claughton.[44] Most of these were small places; only three of them had markets.

These random examples reveal nothing of the size of the shops. It is unlikely that Henry Snape, the bookseller of Astbury in Cheshire,[45] had a stock comparable with that of Roger Ward, the Shrewsbury bookseller who had 2,500 volumes comprising some five hundred titles in stock in 1585.[46] But it would be wrong to assume that shops in small places were necessarily small shops with a limited stock. The inventory of James Backhouse, a shopkeeper of Kirkby Lonsdale who died in 1578, reveals a very large and varied stock. It included almost every conceivable type of cloth in a wide range of colours: kersey, friezado, bays, mockado, borato, camlet, bustian, fustian, rash, buckram, sarsenet, cambric, lawn, linen, canvas and sackcloth. There were hose and netherstocks, gloves, hats of felt and of silk, taffeta and camlet, pins and needles, points and laces, lace of all types, 'Skotishe bobin syllke', 'Spaynish sylke', 'London sylk', 'Bridgis sylke', French garters and Coventry thread. In addition Backhouse stocked a complete range of groceries; all the dried fruits, the sugar and the spices were there. So, too, was the stationery 'department' with its paper and books. The latter included primers, ABCs, grammars, psalms and catechisms, and Aesop, Terence and Virgil.[47] Kirkby Lonsdale had a fine medieval church and a fine medieval bridge attributed to the Devil, but in Backhouse's day, and for centuries after, it was a small market town only thirteen miles from its big neighbour, Kendal. If Backhouse's shop was the village store, its contents would not have disgraced a York or Exeter or perhaps even a London shopkeeper. If it had a window display, it might even satisfy Miss Deane's austere criteria for those fixed retail shops confined to the larger towns.

The example of James Backhouse raises the wider question of how far provincial shops were specialised in this period. Clearly the craftsman retailer was specialised, but what of the mercer or draper or grocer? What, if anything, did these descriptions mean? Often they did not mean that the shopkeeper sold only mercery or drapery or grocery wares. Backhouse's stock suggests a shop of three departments (to use an anachronistic term); one selling mercery and drapery, one selling groceries and one selling stationery. This combination was not uncommon. Thus Thomas Pasmore of Richmond, who died in 1578, had a stock similar to though much smaller than Backhouse's. It, too, included a variety of cloth and hats, spices and dried fruits and paper and books.[48] John Farbeck, a mercer of Durham who died in 1597, had the same mixture of goods; they included such expensive items as $8\frac{1}{4}$ yds of 'French colored velvet', valued at £5 7s, and $\frac{3}{4}$ oz 'Venus gold and silver' at 4s. His total personal estate came to £373 8s 10d.[49] In this sort of combination the stationery department was by far the least important. Thus Thomas Hardman, a Manchester mercer who died in 1583, had a shop in Manchester which contained a great variety of cloth and mercery wares, a limited range of groceries and some paper and primers. The goods in his shop were valued at £293 13s 4d and in his warehouse at £73 7s 6d. He also had a shop at Warrington where the goods were valued at £223 7s 11d; they were mostly cloth with some groceries and paper.[50] When the stationery department dropped out altogether the result was a fairly common combination of mercery and drapery with groceries. This was the case with Edward Hanson, a Manchester mercer and grocer who died in 1584. His two shops, one in Manchester and the other in Bolton, each contained cloth, haberdashery wares and groceries.[51] The same was true of John Johnson of Durham whose mixed stock was valued at £132 3s 1d in 1592.[52] The specialised shop did, of course, exist. William Awyn, a Manchester draper who died in 1590, sold only cottons, friezes and kerseys. The long list of debts owed to him shows that he sold much on credit.[53] Similarly William Watson, a Durham draper, had only cloth in his shop at his death in 1566. There were seventy-four pieces in all, ranging in length from $\frac{1}{2}$ yd to 27 yds; with the chests and cupboards to store them in they were valued at £114 10s.[54] At the other end of the scale was the Kidlington mercer whose inventory of 1581 records 'mercery ware' £2. His total personal estate was worth £3 6s 8d.[55] Perhaps he was a pedlar. Another mercer, John Mondaie of Dudley in Worcestershire who died in 1587, had 'small tryfles of mercery wares' and equipment in his shop valued at only £11, but his inventory shows an interesting side line. His assets included 'raggs for the paper mylne' valued at 10s.[56]

Shops varied from those with a specialised stock to those with a wide and miscellaneous range of goods. In theory specialisation ought to have increased with the size of the town, but there is really not enough evidence as yet to establish such a correlation. The range of goods available in many shops is very impressive. It is difficult to tell how many of these goods had been imported. Were the French garters really from France or did the 'French' denote a style or a means of impressing the customers? Was Backhouse's 'Spaynishe taffetye' really from Spain or was it an English imitation? It is difficult to say. The more expensive cloths and trimmings were probably imported; the silks certainly were. With the groceries there is no doubt: most of the stuff did not grow in this country. The groceries were almost wholly imported. It is misleading to regard shops with a wide range of goods as general stores. They were never quite that, for their stocks did not cover all types of goods.[57] The most notable omission was hardware, which was sold by pewterers, smiths, braziers and ironmongers, all of whom are more elusive than mercers, drapers and grocers. Even if small places had general or village stores, it is curious to regard these as a primitive form of retailing when the present trend is towards the big departmental store, which is only the village store writ large.

Shops might or might not be specialised, but what of the shopkeeper? Was he solely a retailer or did he combine retailing with other occupations? Obviously the craftsman retailer combined retailing with manufacture, and it is sometimes assumed that other retailers 'played an important role in the preparation and processing of the goods they sold'.[58] There seems little evidence of this beyond the obvious 'packaging' of goods which had been bought wholesale in bulk. There is no doubt that shopkeepers engaged in foreign trade. In 1560 the York Merchant Adventurers declared that if they were not allowed to be retailers they would be 'forced to shutt in our shopps'.[59] At Chester a long dispute between the mere merchants and the retailers was settled in 1589 by allowing the mere merchants to retail in one trade and the retailers to trade overseas.[60] At small ports the distinction between mere merchants and retailers could not possibly be maintained, for their foreign trade was insufficient to sustain a class of mere merchants. Even in London merchants who engaged in foreign trade also kept shops;[61] Michael Hicks, 'England's greatest shopkeeper', engaged in foreign trade while he retailed mercery from his shop in Cheapside.[62] In inland towns retailers could find other outlets in the cloth industry. This was certainly so in Lancashire. Thus Lawrence Parker of Colne, who retailed haberdashery wares, was also a small-scale wool dealer. John Lees (or Leese) of Manchester, who died in 1598, had a shop in which he sold cloth in small quantities, but he called himself a clothworker and was engaged in cloth finishing and dyeing. Similarly Manchester shopkeepers combined retailing with the sale of flax and linen yarn.[63] It would be interesting to know whether this diversification occurred in other cloth areas, and especially whether, under the putting-out system, shopkeepers acted as agents of the clothiers by distributing yarn and collecting the cloth from the weavers.

Another diversification of interest and activity for the shopkeeper was agriculture. For one sort of retailers, the butchers, the link between their trade and farming was obvious. For others it is less obvious, though the connection was often there. How often it is difficult to say. In Worcester, for example, neither craftsmen nor shopkeepers seem in general to have engaged in agriculture, but Worcester was a fair-sized town of perhaps four thousand inhabitants; it was deeply involved in the cloth industry and had no cultivated common fields.[64] The limited evidence for Banbury suggests only a modest interest in farming by craftsmen and traders.[65] Further north, in Lancashire and the West Riding, the cloth industry was closely linked with agriculture, but that is hardly surprising with a rural industry. The link was found in towns too. In Manchester clothiers and clothworkers had usually some farming interests, but generally their farming activities were on a limited scale. That was true also of Manchester shopkeepers as their probate inventories show.[66] Edward Hanson, mercer and grocer, had no animals except a gelding, used perhaps for travelling between his Manchester and Bolton shops. Two butchers, Edward Dyson and Robert Wharmby, had only pigs. John Shaw, mercer, had five swine and a horse. Thomas Hardman, another mercer, had three horses, two cows and two swine. Robert Birch, a wealthy linen draper who traded in linen yarn, had '2 kyne and a heffer' and a 'nag'; he seems to have leased a farm out at Lostock. All this could be expected in a place like Manchester which had fields in and around the central township and had a common at Collyhurst to which pigs were supposed to be driven every day.[67] It is indeed rather surprising that Manchester shopkeepers had such a limited interest in agriculture. Perhaps there has been a tendency to exaggerate the town-dwellers' links with farming.

These general and rather superficial observations on shops and shopkeepers may perhaps be given more substance by considering the case of an individual shopkeeper, some of whose accounts have survived and have indeed long been in print. The accounts relate to William Wray, a mercer of Ripon, and they cover the years 1580–99.[68] Little is known about Wray apart from his accounts. He may have been the William Wray who was born in 1552, but that is more likely to have been his son. He was certainly wakeman (the equivalent of mayor) of Ripon in 1584, and he died in 1599. He may have retired from business before his death, for he died at his farm at Hob Green some four miles from Ripon and his probate inventory makes no mention of mercery wares or of a shop. His personal estate was valued at £33 1s 5d after deduction of debts, which included one to his maidservant and one to his manservant. It is possible that the shop had been taken over by Wray's son, who seems to have kept the accounts, but there is no proof of this.

The accounts are confused and disorderly. They are not so much accounts as a sort of day book in which were recorded purchases of stock and the sale of goods that were sold on credit. Wray's pattern of trade conformed fairly closely to that revealed in static form by so many inventories; it was the retailer's classic three-field system (so to speak) of drapery/mercery/haberdashery with groceries and stationery, though in this case the stationery was pretty fallow. The most important section was the first. Ignoring differences of size, colour and quality, Wray stocked about twenty different types of cloth. None of these was the native kersey, dozen or broadcloth. They included harden sold at $4\frac{1}{2}d$ to 7d a yard, canvas usually sold at 1s 4d to 3s 10d a yard, linen, cambric, calico, bays, bombasine and silk (usually sarsenet and silk rash, the latter bought at 33s to 40s the piece). The most important cloths, however, were buffin, durance, fustian, sacking and taffeta. Buffin was 'a coarse cloth in use for gowns';[69] it came in a variety of colours, of which black was the most popular, followed by purple and green. Wray usually bought it at 16s to 18s a piece. Durance, a hard-wearing woollen cloth, was almost invariably 'cremosyne' and cost 27s to 33s a piece wholesale. Fustian, which was usually made from a linen warp and a cotton weft, was variously described as Milan, Jean (Genoa), and Holmes (Ulm) fustian. It was presumably imported and could be expensive, reaching a wholesale price of £4 2s a piece for Milan and £2 a piece for Holmes. 'Seckynge' or sacking was a dress fabric, not the modern sacking. It could be white, striped, 'checker' or coloured (the most popular variety was straw-coloured). It normally cost 20s to 24s a piece wholesale. Finally taffeta, which could be of silk or linen and was sometimes described as Levant or Spanish, varied greatly in price. It could cost the customer anything from 2s to 6s a yard. It was sometimes sold by the nail.

Though Wray sold a few hats and some hose, like other mercers he did not usually sell clothes, but the things necessary for making them. Apart from cloth, these included pins and thread. The latter was bought and sold by weight; Wray normally paid about 1s 6d lb for thread but Coventry thread cost him from 3s to 6s 4d lb and the rather mysterious 'sisters' thread cost as much as £1 lb. Fringe, too, was bought and sold by weight; much of it was black, and it usually cost Wray 3s to 4s lb. Silk, either by weight or by skein, was much more expensive; it was often sold to customers at 2s 6d oz. Lace was stocked in a variety of types and prices, but it is often difficult to tell whether lace or laces was meant.[70] Whatever the abbreviated entries mean, some of the lace or laces was expensive, especially if silk was involved. That was true of points too; a gross of silk points cost 7s to 8s wholesale, compared with 1s 4d to 1s 8d for thread points. Ribbon, gartering and incle were also varied in type and price, and so were buttons. There were silk, hair, thread, corded and tufted buttons; hair and thread buttons cost as little as 6d a gross wholesale, but Wray paid 12s for a dozen silk and gold long buttons.

Wray's trade in groceries, like his trade in mercery wares, reflected closely the sort of stocks recorded in probate inventories. There were the usual dried fruits: currants (sold at 4d to 6d lb), raisins (4d lb), and prunes (3d lb); sugar (selling at the high price of 1s to 2s lb), comfits and candy; pepper (4s lb); cinnamon (6d to 10d oz), ginger (2d to 3d oz), mace (1s oz), cloves (8d to 10d oz); soap and starch, nutmegs, şaffron, turnsole and sanders. There were also gunpowder and cornpowder, though these were hardly groceries. Nor could they be classified as stationery to give some variety to that diminutive 'department', which seems to have sold only brown and white paper, some primers and some 'knots' of minikins or lute strings.

It is easy to see what goods Wray dealt in; it is more difficult to discover where he got them from, though on this the accounts give more information than can usually be obtained from probate inventories. In the 1590s, when the accounts seem more complete, Wray got his goods from about twenty suppliers, most of whom are mere names. Some of the suppliers may have been producers of the goods. Thus soap was bought by the barrel or half barrel from Cecily Sunter, some cloth from William Battie, webster, and 'Lambert wife' of Killinghall, and starch from Robert Barneby of

Newbiggin. Other suppliers were presumably wholesalers. There was pepper from Alderman Richardson of York, Coventry thread and fringe from 'a Coventre man', durance and buffin from John Sill, a Norwich man, fustian, London silk and laces from 'my brother' Walter Dougell, and sacking, incle, thread and buttons from Thomas and Robert Gledell. All these were small suppliers; there were half a dozen bigger men. William, Robert and Ralph Egglefield or Eatenfield[71] supplied a variety of cloth and haberdashery. James Bankes, a linen draper of Ripon, supplied cloth, none of which was linen; whether he was a wholesaler and retailer is not clear. Finally two of the biggest suppliers seem to have been Beverley men. John Gill supplied Wray with a good deal of buffin and durance, some of which was described as bought 'at Baverlaye'. Miles Burton also supplied much buffin and other cloth, and on one occasion Wray arranged to pay a debt to him 'at Beverlay faire next', which rather suggests that he was a Beverley man. There is no evidence that Wray himself bought or sold at Beverley Fair. Indeed he bought in fairly small quantities throughout the year. Thus in 1593 he bought goods on sixteen occasions, in 1594 on twenty occasions and in 1595 on some twenty-six occasions.

Wray paid for many of his purchases immediately or as he put it 'payed and quit', but often he bought on credit or partly on credit. There was usually a down payment of part of the purchase price and the remainder was paid off in anything from a week to a year. Thus on 23 June 1596 he bought cloth and fringe from John Gill for £6 4s, of which £4 was 'payd in part' and the remainder was paid on 23 December 1596. Sometimes the deferred payments were in instalments; buffin and fringe bought from John Gill for £3 12s on 6 April 1598 were paid for as follows: 10s at once, £1 2s on 23 August, £1 on 20 November and £1 on 29 March 1599. This seems to have been unusually long credit; a month to six months was the more common period. The fact that cash and credit purchases were recorded might imply that the accounts give Wray's total purchases and so provide some measure of his turnover. Unfortunately it seems almost certain that the accounts do not give a complete picture, for some of the items sold, especially groceries, do not seem to have any corresponding entries for purchases. For what they are worth, the figures for purchases in the 1590s were as follows: 1590 £32 1s 4d; 1591 £41 7s 10d; 1592

£17 3s 2d; 1593 £44 1s 5d; 1594 £55 12s 5d; 1595 £67 12s 5d; 1596 £36 10s 1d; 1597 £36 2s 8d; 1598 £21 2s 4d. These figures give an annual average of just over £39, which seems low.

These figures would have more meaning if it were possible to calculate the profit margin on which Wray operated. In theory this should be possibly by comparing his buying and selling prices, but in practice this is very difficult. For example he normally bought cloth by the piece of unspecified length and sold it by the yard. In only some half a dozen cases can the comparison be made with reasonable safety. Thus Wray usually bought black buffin at 16s a piece, and he sold a piece for 19s, an increase of 19 per cent. Milan fustian bought in the half piece at 2s 8d yd was apparently sold for 4s yd, an increase of 40 per cent. The same seems to have been true of silk rash. Levant taffeta, bought at 1s 5d yd, was sold at 2s yd, an increase of 41 per cent. One would expect the margin to be greater when a piece was cut up for sale, as there might be some wastage. Of groceries, mace was bought at 9d oz and sold at 1s oz, and prunes, bought at just over 2d lb, were sold at 3d. It would be difficult to draw any firm conclusions from such examples, but the impression that, in this sort of trade, retail prices were in general a third higher than wholesale prices may not be far wrong. On this assumption Wray's average outlay of £39 per annum would yield a gross profit (before expenses) of £13 per annum. This seems much too small; it is almost exactly what a master mason or carpenter could legally earn under the East Riding wage assessment of 1593.[72] The only reasonable explanation of this is that the accounts do not record all Wray's purchases and therefore underestimate his trade and his profits.

At least it is clear that the accounts do not record all Wray's sales. They record some goods sold on credit and some debts owed to Wray; the latter include debts for unspecified wares, but they also include debts arising from money lending. This record is plainly incomplete, but it is useful in providing some information on Wray's customers. These naturally included people in Ripon itself; John Fawcet of Skelgate who owed 19s for wares and 'money lent'; Robert Rokyng's wife of Bondgate who owed 2s 3d for wares; Simon Askew or Ascough, wakeman in 1600, who bought cloth and groceries, and so on. More interesting were the country customers for they give some idea of the geographical range of Wray's trade. The most important of these were Sir

William Mallory and his son John of Studley Royal and Hutton Conyers. They bought cloth, groceries, haberdashery and gunpowder in considerable quantities. For this they had a running account with Wray which was always in arrears, but at least he could claim a share of the carriage trade. There were a few distant customers, for whom there may have been special reasons. Thus William Meres of Leeds bought small quantities of cloth, buttons, silk and lute strings in 1580; he was described as 'sometime Sir. Robt. Owtherit man', and a Sir Robert Outhwaite was among Wray's debtors. In general the country customers lived within a radius of ten miles round Ripon and the majority of them were within six miles of the town. Some of these country customers came to town to do their shopping on a Thursday, which was market day; Mr Wilson of Tanfield was doing this in the summer of 1587. But it must be admitted that they shopped on any day of the week, for if the dates can be believed the shop was open on a Sunday.

Just as Wray's purchases and sales reveal a range of goods that can be paralleled from the stock listed in probate inventories, so too can his trade with country customers be paralleled by the evidence of debts recorded in such inventories. Thus William Awyn, the Manchester draper who died in 1590, was owed money for goods supplied to customers in Mottram, Carrington (Cheshire), Clifton, Ordsall and Pendleton. Other Manchester shopkeepers were owed money by people in a much wider range of places than this, but it is often uncertain whether the money was owed for goods or for loans. Perhaps the distinction is not really important, for the very existence of such debts shows an economic relationship between the urban shopkeeper and his country hinterland. This relationship between an urban centre and the surrounding countryside is important in the study of retail trade where it is desirable to define marketing areas. The nature of the sources makes this a difficult task, but a happy combination of sources can give fruitful results as Professor Rodgers has shown in his work on Preston. Using largely the evidence of out-of-town stallengers and out-burgesses, he found that Preston had a market area with an inner zone varying in radius from seven to twelve miles and an irregular outer zone that could extend to twenty miles. Most of the stallengers and out-burgesses lived within seven miles of Preson and most of the traceable commercial transactions fell within that limit.[73] In a very small way Wray's country customers seem to present a similar pattern.

It is probable that the marketing area of the individual customer varied with his economic and social status: the lower the status the narrower the area. Unfortunately the evidence for individual buying habits is almost confined to the gentry. Only in their household accounts is it possible to see the full range of sources that an individual drew upon for his consumer goods. If the Shuttleworths may once again be taken as an example, it seems that they drew on all available sources. Their dealings with pedlars were slight, but they made much fuller use of fairs and probably of markets, not only for buying household provisions but also for buying farm stock and selling grain. They made use of the craftsman-retailer too, buying shoes from a shoemaker in Burnley and saddles and bridles from a saddler in Wigan.[74] Though the accounts do not say that goods were bought in shops, many of the purchases in Manchester, Warrington, Chester and elsewhere must have been made in shops there. Indeed one of the features of the accounts is the sheer range of places at which purchases were made. All this was in addition to the supplies from the home farm. The Shuttleworths slaughtered their own meat, paying a butcher 3d to do the job, but they also bought mutton, lamb and veal, often in Manchester.[75] Finally they received a good deal of food as gifts from friends and neighbours. It would be misleading to regard this as free, for two reasons. Firstly it must be assumed that such gifts were reciprocated and secondly they involved the payment of handsome tips to the servants bringing the gifts. No doubt such tips depended on the size and weight of the gift, the distance it had to be brought and the status of its giver and of its recipient. Whatever subtle combination of effort and social custom decided the size of the tips, they were surprisingly large. In 1584 'a mayed of Thomas Kenyam which did bringe apples and halfe a dowsane chikenes' was given 6d, and 'Rychard Urmestone man which brought a presente frome him' was given 1s (he had probably come from West Leigh, about seven miles).[76] Such sums may not appear large, but at that time the Shuttleworths were paying the slater 4d a day, though he probably got meat and drink in addition (so probably did the bringers of presents). Tips of this size were common. In the case of men the modern equivalent in comparison with wages might be £5 or more. The men bringing presents of bucks were usually given 6s 8d,[77] which was more than a craftsman earned in a week. The Shuttleworths were not alone in giving large tips. In the early seventeenth century the Howards of Naworth Castle were even more lavish; they regularly rewarded the bringers of presents with sums that were two to four times as large as the daily wage they were paying to their labourers.[78] It was a curious practice, deeply embedded in a paternalistic view of social and economic relationships, and it would merit more examination within the context of those relationships.

The Shuttleworths were Lancashire gentry, and their shopping habits were probably typical of their time, place and social standing. What they did not themselves produce, they bought from the variety of sources available to the consumer with money to spend. Lower down the social scale choice must have been more restricted. For many goods the restriction must have come from the side of demand rather than supply, from price rather than opportunity. The market for costly imported fabrics and the more expensive groceries must have been a restricted one, but such things were available locally to those who could afford to buy them. In 1561–2 Edward, Earl of Derby, paid £59 11s 8d 'for spices bought in Lancashire',[79] but no one else in the county could afford to buy on that scale. The purchases of those much lower in the social scale are more difficult to assess. Contemporaries commented on what they regarded as the increasing luxury of the age, but luxury was too strong a word, except perhaps as applied to the aristocracy. It was not so much luxury as more privacy, more comfort and more variety that men sought. This was reflected in the countryside by 'the great rebuilding' of farmhouses.[80] It was reflected in town and country by the contents of the houses that inventories reveal; less perhaps in the actual furniture than in the pewter and plate, the feather beds and the linen. No doubt there were limits to this. Probate inventories are a biased sample which largely ignores the poor. Nevertheless some branches of retailing, especially the shops, do seem to reflect a demand, perhaps a growing demand, from some sections of the community for a variety of goods which were often by no means cheap. The stocks of some provincial shopkeepers only seem intelligible in this sort of context.

Notes

[1] N. S. B. Gras, *The evolution of the English corn market* (1926); P. J. Bowden, *The wool trade in Tudor and Stuart England* (1962); J. U. Nef, *The rise of the British coal industry* (1932).

[2] Harrison, 'Description', p. 274.

[3] T. Wilson, *A discourse upon usury*, ed. R. H. Tawney, p. 203.

[4] P. Stubbes, *The anatomie of abuses*, ed. F. J. Furnivall (New Shakspere Society), part II, pp. 24–6.

[5] Cotton MSS., Tib. D. viii, f. 51 (British Museum). These undated but Elizabethan 'priviledges graunted to the Englishe merchanttes in Andwerpe' have never been printed. For another version of the restrictions on retailers see W. E. Lingelbach, ed., *The Merchant Adventurers of England. Their laws and ordinances*, pp. 111–14.

[6] P. Croft, ed., *The Spanish Company*, London Record Soc., ix (1973), p. 91.

[7] 3/4 Ed. vi. c. 21.

[8] Especially in Professor Everitt's fine chapter on 'The marketing of agricultural produce' in J. Thirsk, ed., *The agrarian history of England and Wales*, iv. ch. viii. See also M. J. Hodgen, 'Fairs of Elizabethan England', *Economic Geography*, xviii (1942), 389–400.

[9] A. D. Dyer, *The city of Worcester in the sixteenth century*, p. 79.

[10] *Shuttleworth accounts*, i. 54–5, 100, 114; J. Humphreys, 'Elizabethan estate book of Grafton Manor', *Trans. Birmingham Arch. Soc.*, xliv (1920), 58; W. Stevenson, 'Extracts from "The booke of the howshold charges and other paiments laid out by the L. North"', *Archaeologia*, xix (1821), 291–5.

[11] F. G. Emmison, *Tudor Secretary. Sir William Petre at Court and home*, pp. 148–58.

[12] J. Thirsk, ed., *op. cit.*, iv. 496–8.

[13] 5/6 Ed. vi. c. 21.

[14] Lansdowne MSS., 105 No. 53 (British Museum).

[15] J. P. Earwaker, ed., *The Court Leet records of the Manor of Manchester*, i. 59–60.

[16] F. W. Dendy, ed., *Extracts from the records of the Merchant Adventurers of Newcastle-upon-Tyne*, Surtees Society, xciii (1894), i. 54, 97, 98 n.

[17] *Shuttleworth accounts*, i. 134.

[18] G. Ornsby, ed., *Selections from the household books of Lord*

William Howard of Naworth Castle, Surtees Society, lxviii (1877), 10.

[19] J. T. Fowler, 'The account-book of William Wray', *The Antiquary*, xxxii (1896), 117.

[20] *Ibid.*, p. 56.

[21] P. Croft, ed., *The Spanish Company*, London Record Soc., ix (1973), p. 91.

[22] F. C. Morgan, 'Trade in Hereford in the 16th century', *Trans. Woolhope Naturalists' Field Club* (1936–8), p. 17.

[23] An exception is A. D. Dyer, *The city of Worcester in the sixteenth century*, ch. 10.

[24] M. A. Havinden, ed., *Household and farm inventories in Oxfordshire, 1550–1590*, pp. 67–9, 86–7.

[25] M. Cash, ed., *Devon inventories of the sixteenth and seventeenth centuries*, Devon and Cornwall Record Soc., n.s. xi (1966), 7.

[26] A. D. Dyer, ed., 'Probate inventories of Worcester tradesmen, 1545–1614', *Worcestershire Historical Soc.*, n.s., 5, Miscellany II (1967), pp. 30–2. For further evidence of shoemakers and their stock see D. M. Woodward, 'The Chester leather industry, 1558–1625', *Trans. Historic Soc. of Lancs. and Cheshire*, 119 (1967), pp. 65–111.

[27] F. G. Emmison, *Elizabethan life: disorder*, p. 263.

[28] H. V. F. Somerset, 'An account book of an Oxford undergraduate in the years 1619–1622', *Oxoniensia*, xxii (1957), 85–92.

[29] Havinden, *op. cit.*, pp. 143–4.

[30] J. C. Hodgson, ed., *Wills and inventories*, pt. III, Surtees Soc. cxii (1906), p. 152.

[31] D. M. Woodward, 'The Chester leather industry', *Trans. Historic Soc. of Lancs. and Cheshire*, 119 (1967), p. 79.

[32] J. Raine, ed., *Wills and inventories*, pt. I, Surtees Society, ii (1835), 310.

[33] A. D. Dyer, ed., 'Probate inventories of Worcester tradesmen', *Worcestershire Historical Soc.*, n.s., 5, Miscellany II (1967), pp. 25–8.

[34] J. C. Hodgson, ed., *op. cit.*, p. 93.

[35] Inventory in L.R.O.

[36] D. M. Woodward, 'The Chester leather industry', p. 96.

[37] Dorothy Davis, *A history of shopping* (1966).

[38] Phyllis Deane, *The first Industrial Revolution*, pp. 257–8.

[39] D. W. Woodward, 'Freemen's rolls', *The local historian*, 9 (1970), pp. 89–95.

[40] E. Rideout, 'The Chester Companies and the Old Quay', *Trans. of Lancs. and Cheshire Historic Soc.*, 79 (1928), pp. 141–74.

[41] J. F. Pound, 'The social and trade structure of Norwich, 1525–1575', *Past and Present*, 34 (1966), p. 60.

[42] E. Arber, ed., *A transcript of the Registers of the Company of Stationers of London*, II *passim*.

[43] B. Marsh, ed., *Records of the Worshipful Company of Carpenters*, iii, 163; iv (ed. J. Ainsworth), 157, 184, 204.

[44] J. Tait, ed., *Lancashire Quarter Sessions Records*, i, Chetham Society, n.s., 77 (1917), *passim*.

[45] E. Arber, *op. cit.*, ii. 138.

[46] H. S. Bennett, *English books and readers 1558–1603*, pp. 71, 264–5; A. Rodger, 'Roger Ward's Shrewsbury stock: an inventory of 1585', *The Library*, 5th ser., xiii (1958), 247–68.

[47] J. Raine, ed., *Wills and inventories from the Registry of the Archdeaconry of Richmond*, Surtees Soc., xxvi (1853), 275–81. The printed version of the inventory is not quite complete, but even so it fills five printed pages.

[48] *Ibid.*, pp. 268–70. Pasmore's 'pentesse' was valued at 6s.

[49] *Ibid.*, pt. II, Surtees Soc., xxxviii (1860), 281–3.

[50] Inventory in L.R.O.

[51] Inventory in L.R.O.

[52] J. Raine, ed., *op. cit.*, pp. 210–13. His stock did include one ream of paper.

[53] Inventory in L.R.O.

[54] J. Raine, ed., *Wills and inventories*, pt. I, Surtees Soc., ii (1835), 253–9.

[55] Havinden, *op. cit.*, p. 125.

[56] J. S. Roper, ed., *Dudley probate inventories, 1544–1603*, p. 45.

[57] For some interesting examples of this see L. B. and M. W. Barley, 'Lincolnshire shopkeepers in the sixteenth and seventeenth centuries', *The Lincolnshire Historian*, II (1962), 7–21.

[58] P. Deane, *The first Industrial Revolution*, p. 258.

[59] M. Sellers, ed., *The York Mercers and Merchant Adventurers, 1356–1917*, Surtees Soc., cxxix (1917), 165.

[60] D. M. Woodward, *The trade of Elizabethan Chester*, p. 101.

[61] T. S. Willan, *The Muscovy merchants of 1555*, p. 45.

[62] R. G. Lang, 'London's aldermen in business: 1600–1625', *The Guildhall Miscellany*, iii (1971), 247.

[63] N. Lowe, *The Lancashire textile industry in the sixteenth century*, Chetham Society, 3rd ser., xx (1972), 24, 36, 49.

[64] A. D. Dyer, *The city of Worcester in the sixteenth century*, pp. 133–4.

[65] See the Banbury inventories in Havinden, *op. cit.*

[66] The inventories referred to are in L.R.O.

[67] J. P. Earwaker, ed., *The Court Leet records of the Manor of Manchester*, i. 15, ii, 93.

[68] J. T. Fowler, ed., 'The account-book of William Wray', *The Antiquary*, xxxii (1896), 54–7, 76–81, 117–20, 178–80, 212–14, 242–4, 278–81, 316–17, 346–7, 369–75. It does not seem necessary to give detailed references to these accounts.

[69] *O.E.D.*

[70] The editor of the accounts assumes that all references to lace meant laces, but this seems doubtful.

[71] William and Ralph were brothers.

[72] P. L. Hughes and J. F. Larkin, eds. *Tudor royal proclamations*, iii. 122–5.

[73] H. B. Rodgers, 'The market area of Preston in the sixteenth and seventeenth centuries', *Geographical Studies*, iii (1956), 45–55.

[74] *Shuttleworth accounts*, i. 106–7, 112.

[75] *Ibid.*, i. 10, 37, 72.

[76] *Ibid.*, i. 19–20.

[77] *Ibid.*, i. 113.

[78] G. Ornsby, ed., *Selections from the household books of Lord Howard of Naworth Castle*, Surtees Soc., lxviii (1877), 26–33. For other examples of large-scale presents of food see J. Evans, 'An account of the presents received and expenses incurred at the wedding of Richard Polsted, of Albury, Esquire', *Archaeologia*, 36 (1855), pp. 33–52; W. D. Cooper, ed., 'The expenses of the Judges of Assize riding the Western and Oxford circuits, temp. Elizabeth', *Camden Miscellany* iv (Camden Society, lxxiii, 1858).

[79] F. R. Raines, ed., *The Stanley papers*, pt. II, Chetham Society, xxxi (1853), 2.

[80] W. G. Hoskins, *Provincial England*, pp. 131–48.

III PROVINCIAL SHOPS IN THE SEVENTEENTH CENTURY

The Elizabethan pattern of retail trade was maintained during the seventeenth century, but the sources for studying that trade remain scanty and scattered. This is especially true of the provincial trade as represented by fairs and markets, pedlars and retailing craftsmen. In general the evidence is perhaps slightly fuller than for the previous century. There are more household accounts and more comments by travellers; the probate inventories are more numerous and still informative; there are even one or two diaries or memoirs of retailers and there are hundreds of trade tokens issued by shopkeepers. All these are helpful, but one would willingly barter some of them for the actual business records of even a handful of retailers or for the sort of directories that were published in the later eighteenth century.

The picture this evidence reveals is the familiar one showing a variety of sources from which the consumer could obtain his goods. The large households of the gentry continued to buy some of their supplies from fairs. The Shuttleworths, now residing at the newly built Gawthorpe Hall near Burnley, still bought some fish and hops at Stourbridge Fair; in 1621 they were brought in a pack to Preston at a cost in carriage of 15s.[1] But such purchases seem to have been rare in comparison with the grocery, mercery and haberdashery wares which were bought in London and brought by carrier to Halifax.[2] The Howards of Naworth got their fish at Morpeth, Newcastle, Workington and Hartlepool,[3] but they bought groceries, hops and lawn at the St Luke's and Lammas Fairs at Newcastle,[4] and candlesticks, basins, salts and brass pots at Carlisle where they traded in their old pewter and brass.[5] Later in the century Sir Thomas Haggerston of Haggerston (some six miles south-east of Berwick upon Tweed) was buying wooden vessels at Weetwood Fair, brass weights and seals for his wife and cloth at St Ninian's Fair at Fenton, and 'prospective glasses' and 'night gowne, pety coate, gloves and gartars' at Newcastle Fair.[6] Such purchases were much less important than the regular supplies of groceries from Newcastle. In general this retail trading must have been of minor significance to the fairs in comparison with their wholesale trade and their trade in farm stock. It is surely significant that, at the Cross Fair at Beverley, the week before Holy Thursday was called 'whole sale weeke', and on Holy Thursday, 'the great fayre day', the Londoners went 'most of them away'.[7] It is probable that the main contribution of fairs to the retail trade was in providing a source of supply for shopkeepers.[8]

Fairs were probably of minor importance as a source of supply for the ordinary consumer. As before, he was more likely to look to the weekly market, but on this there is little precise information. The accounts of journeys written by an increasing number of travellers show that the state of the local market was one of the criteria used in judging the merits of a town. In 1681 Thomas Baskerville found the market place at Norwich full of provisions, especially on Saturdays,[9] and Celia Fiennes noted the 'very large market place and hall and cross for fruite and little things every day'.[10] She found 'provisions very plentifull and cheap' in the market at Ripon, while at Chesterfield and Maidstone the markets were so well furnished they were 'like some little faire'. At Tunbridge Wells in 1697 the company staying for the waters bought their provisions 'at the market which is just by the Wells and furnish'd with great plenty of all sorts of flesh fowle and fish . . . as also the country people come with all their back yard and barne door affords to supply them with, and their gardens and orchards which makes the markets well stored and provision cheape'. It sounds the ideal market, only slightly marred by the souvenir shops with their toys, silver, china and 'curious wooden ware' on the other side of the 'Walk'.[11]

Markets continued to be important, and pedlars continued to peddle in their usual obscurity. One type of specialised pedlar, the glassman who wandered up and down the country selling glasses, was classified as a rogue by an Act of 1604,[12] but that did not stop him. In 1614 at Kirdford in Sussex a glass carrier had six small nags and a cart,[13] and in 1619 the Howards of Naworth were buying glasses 'at the gate'.[14] Later in the century Sarah Fell of Swarthmoor Hall was selling her rabbit skins at 2d each to Tom Atkinson, 'pedler', and buying from him ribbon, laces, silk and tape for herself, her sister and her servant. She also got the same sort of haberdashery from a shop in Ulverston.[15] About the same time Daniel Fleming of Rydal Hall was buying books, including bibles, a razor, cloth, laces, silk and combs from pedlars, one of whom was described as 'the Lancashire pedler'.[16] Similarly in the 1690s Sir Thomas Haggerston was getting goods from Berwick, Newcastle, London and Edinburgh and buying his 'chawing tobaco' at Mr Lamb's in Durham (at 3s lb), but he was also getting 'large sissers', lace, girth web, muslin and 'washt leather riding gloves' from a number of pedlars. They included 'Stuart the pedlar', who supplied lace and holland cloth, probably from over the border.[17] Unfortunately it is impossible to tell how dependent less exalted consumers were on the services of the pedlar.

Pedlars themselves were still regarded with some hostility by other retailers. There were a number of Bills 'against hawkers and pedlars' in the House of Commons in the 1690s, which apparently aimed at their suppression.[18] None became law, but in 1697 hawkers, pedlars and petty chapmen were made subject to a tax of £4; they were to pay another £4 for every horse, ass or mule they used in their business.[19] The purpose of this was purely fiscal; it was part of the increasing taxation to pay for the war, and unfortunately it occasioned no debate on the activities and numbers of pedlars. Though retailers in general may have been hostile to pedlars, there is still some slight evidence that shopkeepers supplied pedlars with goods. In 1663 Roger Lowe, who managed a shop at Ashton-in-Markerfield, had dealings with Humphrey Starbotham, a pedlar living in Wigan, which suggest that he was supplying Starbotham with goods on credit.[20] Similarly Henry Best of Emswell in the East Riding reported in 1641 that huswife cloth was 'broughte aboute of peddlers, whoe furnish themselves thereof in Cleaveland, and Blakeamoore, wheare they buy very much of this sorte'. These pedlars may have bought direct from the makers, but a finer linen called holland cloth was imported 'by our merchants and solde to our linnen drapers, att whose shoppes our countrey-pedlers furnish themselves'.[21] It is perhaps not surprising that the London linen-drapers opposed a Bill against hawkers and pedlars in December 1692 and petitioned against it, but perhaps they were wholesalers.[22]

The pedlar did not make the goods he sold whereas the craftsman-retailer usually did and often maintained a considerable stock. Thus Ralph Morgan, a Chester shoemaker who died in 1623, had '19 dozen and 3 pairs of shoes which ranged in size from children's shoes and then from size 3 up to size 12 inclusive'.[23] Ten years later a Petworth shoemaker had sixty-three pairs of shoes valued at $9\frac{1}{2}d$ a pair.[24] John Nixon, a Lincoln shoemaker, had boots and shoes valued at £9 19s 6d in 1663.[25] It was perhaps this retailing function that helped a shoemaker in a 'leather' town like Congleton to become mayor in 1623–4 and 1636–7.[26] Though shoemakers often had substantial stocks, they were small in comparison with the stocks needed to supply the army with boots and shoes in the 1640s. In 1642 Northampton seems to have supplied eleven thousand pairs of shoes and six hundred pairs of boots for the forces in Ireland.[27] It would be interesting to know exactly how this was done and whether it was a Sombartian case of 'war and capitalism'. Saddlers, too, continued to act as craftsmen-retailers. William Coates, a Lichfield saddler, had a dozen new saddles in his shop in 1663; Richard Beardsley, another Lichfield saddler, had saddles, harness and whips in his shops at Lichfield and Tamworth in 1666.[28] It seems that some craftsmen developed into more general shopkeepers. Richard Cooke, a Hereford saddler whose goods were seized for debt in 1693, had a large and varied stock in trade. This included saddles, bridles, stirrups, collars, whips and indeed everything connected with furniture for horses. But it also included fish-hooks, besoms, tobacco boxes, holsters, pistols and 'brest plates', nails, chains (for dogs) and shoe buckles. Clearly Cooke did not make all these goods, though he certainly made saddlery. His shop was still centred in saddlery, but it had acquired some of the features of a more general store.[29] This development was also found among chandlers. Robert Mason, a chandler of Lincoln who died in 1627, made candles on a fairly large scale, but he also sold grocery wares and ironmongery and even fish. Three years later James Smyth, a Stamford chandler, was certainly making candles, but they formed a small part of his business. They were less important than the grocery, ironmongery and haberdashery wares in his shop.[30] Here again a general store seems to have developed from the nucleus of a particular craft. It would be interesting to know how common this development was in the transition from the craftsman who sold what he had made to the shopkeeper who sold what others had produced.

When Celia Fiennes visited Derby in 1698 she found it a dear place for strangers and one where 'they had only shops of all sorts of things'. By contrast she found provisions good and cheap at Newcastle upon Tyne where 'their shops are good and are of distinct trades, not selling many things in one shop as is the custom in most country towns and cittys'.[31] Shops may have been more specialised than Miss Fiennes suggested, especially in cities, but many of them were not confined to one type of goods. The combination of drapery, haberdashery and mercery with groceries and stationery persisted. Thus Roger Sankey, who was described as a gentleman and was a mercer with a shop in Ormskirk, had a varied stock at his death in 1613 when his personal estate was valued at £364 0s 6d. His shop contained a wide range of cloths with the usual lace, ribbons, buttons and points, and a good range of groceries with the usual sugar, dried fruits, spices and medicaments. The stationery section had paper and parchment, pens and inkhorns, and a selection of primers, ABCs, Greek grammars, accidences, Catos, Terences and 'Sentences pueriles', some no doubt intended for the pupils at the local grammar school.[32] Matthew Markland, a Wigan mercer who died in 1617, had a similar stock in trade, which was valued for probate at £343 out of a total personal estate of about £1,300. The personal estate included £825 in debts owed to Markland, but it is impossible to tell how many of these were for goods sold on credit.[33] Similarly Thomas Harris, a mercer of Charlbury in Oxfordshire who died in 1632, stocked cloth and haberdashery wares as well as groceries and stationery. As he also sold glasses, pots and jugs, gunpowder and shot, nails and knives, red herrings and sprats, his shop must have been something of a general store. His debts to a London mercer and a London grocer suggest sources of supply for his varied stock.[34] The stock of a Caernarvon mercer in 1673 was even more varied for it included a range of apothecary's wares as well as mercery, haberdashery, groceries, stationery and ironmongery. This stock was valued for probate at about £325.[35]

The evidence of probate inventories suggests that most shops, especially in small places, had a fairly mixed stock in trade, but that the specialised shop, quite apart from the craftsman-retailer, did exist. The ironmonger sometimes kept to his hardware and the draper might confine himself to selling cloth. Thus Michael Hardinge, a Lichfield ironmonger who died in 1662, seems to have had nothing but ironmongery in his shop.[36] William Craig, a draper of Roxwell in Essex, had nothing but cloth in his shop at his death in 1683.[37] John Scholfield, a Manchester woollen draper who died in 1665, had only 'cloath in the shoppe', but it was valued at £322 5s 6d; he may well have been a wholesale draper.[38] Similarly Abraham Hamer of Rochdale, whose personal estate was valued at £1,217 in 1682, was described as a mercer, but his shop contained little but groceries. His very large quantities of sugar in hogsheads and barrels and his 3 tons of oil valued at £108 strongly suggest that he combined wholesaling with retailing.[39] Indeed in many cases it is difficult to tell whether a local trader was a wholesaler or a retailer or perhaps was both. This may be illustrated by the trade of one of the Tench family of Nantwich, a fragment of whose accounts for the years 1615 to 1626 has survived.[40]

The accounts seem to have been kept by Lawrence or Eldred Tench, two of the four sons of John Tench, a dyer of Nantwich.[41] Whichever Tench he was, he engaged in a variety of trading activities. He sold large quantities of groceries to William Moonke and a Mr Young. They were the standard groceries of the period: sugar, pepper, ginger, mace, cloves, currants, raisins, prunes, nutmegs, cinnamon, aniseeds, starch and soap. They were often sold in quantities larger than was usual in the retail trade; currants by the half or quarter hundredweight, prunes and sugar sometimes by the hundredweight and even pepper by the hundredweight (at 1s 8d lb or £9 6s 8d cwt). All this suggests a wholesale trade; even the Scotchman who bought 6½ lb ginger may have been a pedlar. Similarly on 7 December 1615 Tench sold Mr Wixsted thirty-one hats,[42] hat bands, canvas, frieze and grogram, which must surely have been bought for re-sale, unless it was a mourning order. On the other hand Oliver Dekins was sold a hat for himself and one for his son and a rug (a woollen cloth), Roger Boyne was sold two 'gray ruges' for 15s and Robert Wilkinson some ribbon and lace for 16s, which he agreed to pay at 8d a week. These look more like retail sales, though again Wilkinson may have been a pedlar. Tench also dealt in 'slippings' or tow yarn, which was 'put forth to whyting' before being sold, tallow, candles and cheese. He sold the occasional piece of timber and a good many 'treies', 'tries' or 'triees', which were presumably trees which grow and not sieves. They cost anything from 1s 9d to 6s each; perhaps they were for planting. Finally Tench had a trading venture to Ireland in 1618 for which he bought cloth, lace, hemp, cheese and unspecified wares costing £217 17s 11d in all. There is no evidence on the outcome of this venture. Not much can be made of these accounts, which are little more than fragmentary jottings, but they suggest a local trader making money wherever he could without much regard for the type of goods or the type of trade. They are perhaps something of a warning against too rigid a classification into wholesalers and retailers.

The fact that many provincial shops were not highly specialised may have made it easy for them to absorb new products into their stock in trade, and there was one new, or fairly new, product of great importance in this period. That was tobacco. Increasing imports of tobacco brought a dramatic fall in price and led to increased consumption. In 1614 it was said in the House of Commons that 'poor men spend 4d of their day's wages at night in smoke',[43] but in the following year only 60,831 lb of tobacco were imported.[44] This was hardly surprising, for Matthew Markland's meagre stock of tobacco in his Wigan shop was valued at 9s lb in 1617. Seven years later Lady Katherine Paston wrote to her son William at Corpus Christi College, Cambridge, 'I hop to heer you still hate the very smell of tobaca', and sent him juice of liquorice for the 'ruhum', no doubt as an alternative.[45] It was a losing battle against the 'pot' of the day; by 1628 imports reached 672, 692 lb,[46] and in 1632 Thomas Harris's stock of tobacco at Charlbury was valued at 1s 8d lb. Hitherto tobacco retailers had not required a licence, but in 1633 a licensing system was introduced. By 1637 2,063 licences had been granted for England and Wales at an average fee of £5. They were distributed very unevenly; there was a heavy concentration of licences in London and Middlesex and in the south-western counties of Devon, Cornwall and Somerset. Elsewhere the smaller number of licences may have reflected the greater amount of unlicensed trading.[47]

The grant of licences shows that tobacco sellers were numerous, but it does not imply that such sellers sold nothing but tobacco. There were no doubt specialised tobacco dealers in London, and provincial smokers sometimes got their tobacco direct from the capital. On 12 May 1674 Thomas Thelkeld wrote to his kinsman, Christopher Blencowe, from London telling him that he had sent 'by Richard Robinson, carrier of Kendal' 14 lb of 'best Verginia cutt' at 2s 2d lb in a 'wanescot box'. The tobacco could be collected at Penrith in a fortnight, and 'the same party brings you the tobacco' would safely bring Thelkeld the money for it.[48] Such dealings with the capital were clearly not essential, for tobacco was available in the provinces where it does not seem usually to have been sold by specialised retailers. It could be bought from pedlars and from mercers, apothecaries, barbers and even ironmongers. The fact that the expanding tobacco trade was apparently absorbed by existing shopkeepers rather than by the creation of new specialised outlets may be some indication of the number and distribution of shops.

It is in fact very difficult to get any real idea of the number and distribution of provincial shops in this period. This arises from the absence of directories and the fragmentary nature of other evidence. There is however one source which is worth exploring for the light it throws on the number and distribution of shops. This source is the token coinage issued between 1649 and 1672.[44] These tokens were first catalogued by William Boyne in 1858, and a much expanded and revised edition of Boyne was produced by George C. Williamson and published in 1889–91. Williamson's edition has been used in the following analysis of the tokens.[50] A great deal of work has been done on the tokens since 1891[51] and a great many new tokens have come to light since then. Thus Williamson listed seventy-eight different tokens for Oxford, but E. Thurlow Leeds was able to list 113 tokens for the city in 1923;[52] again Williamson listed 308 tokens for Surrey, but about 360 are now known.[53] Many of these tokens that have come to light since Williamson are simply variants of issues that he catalogued. An increase in the number of issues does not imply a proportionate increase in the numbers of issuers. The thirty-five new tokens for Oxford only added two or three to the number of issuers, and it is the number of issuers, not the number of issues, that is important when using tokens as evidence for the distribution of trades.

The tokens issued between 1649 and 1672 were usually of brass or copper, though a few were of lead. They were issued in denominations of $\frac{1}{4}d$, $\frac{1}{2}d$, and $1d$. The penny tokens were practically confined to London, Yorkshire, Cheshire, Shropshire, Lancashire, Wales and Ireland. No satisfactory explanation for this limited distribution of penny tokens has yet been found. The tokens were issued after the withdrawal of the copper farthings that had been issued under patents of James I and Charles I. They were clearly meant to provide small change in the absence of any official copper coinage. It has also been suggested that they provided a form of advertisement for the issuer, and that this was one of the motives of issue. This does not seem a very convincing motive if it is assumed that the geographical distribution of individual issues was limited, which appears likely.[54] It should, however, be remembered that the issue of tokens could be profitable if they were not all returned for conversion into coin of the realm. The intrinsic value of tokens was much less than their face value.

The real mystery about these tokens can only be touched upon here; it is the mystery of who actually made them and in what quantities. Some work has been done on this, but no very satisfactory conclusions seem to have been reached. It is clearly impossible that all tokens should have been made in the places where they were issued; there cannot always have been the local skill for that. It is possible that most of the provincial tokens were made in London. It is known that the London engraver, David Ramage, was responsible for some provincial tokens.[55] Even so, it is not certain whether London supplied simply the dies, or the dies and the blanks, or the entire token. The whole matter needs more investigation. The question of how many tokens were struck for a particular issue is even more difficult. There is no evidence at all on the size of the issues when tokens were issued by individuals. Some tokens, however, were issued by towns which on occasion recorded the cost of the tokens. In a few such cases it is possible to discover the weight of the metal and to divide this by the weight of a surviving token. Using this method it has been calculated that the $\frac{1}{4}d$ token of the city of Oxford in 1652 had an issue of 100,000. The Norwich farthing tokens issued between 1667 and 1670 may have numbered 94,000; they were obtained from London.[56] Smaller places had smaller issues. Sherborne seems to have issued about 58,000 town tokens, Poole about 18,000[57] and Bewdley about 14,000.[58] Williamson listed 12,722 different tokens for the British Isles.[59] If only one thousand of each variety had been issued, the total would exceed twelve millions. It is quite a large figure and might help to explain why so many tokens have survived despite the royal proclamation of 1672 which forbade their circulation. They were replaced by copper farthings and halfpennies issued by the mint.

These trade tokens must now be looked at for the evidence they provide on retail trade. In analysing Williamson's catalogue of them, I have limited myself to provincial England and Wales, omitting Scotland, Ireland, the Isle of Man, London and Southwark.[60] In provincial England and in Wales 7,787 different tokens were issued by 6,575 issuers. These are impressive figures, but more impressive is the fact that tokens were issued in 1,534 places, which is nearly twice as many places as there were market towns in 1640. These places were unevenly distributed. Very few of them were in Wales (thirty-six places for the whole of Wales), Monmouthshire (four), Herefordshire (eight), Rutland (five) and the northern counties of Northumberland (one), Durham (nine), Cumberland (three) and Westmorland (five). The county league table was headed by Kent (103 places), followed by Yorkshire (ninety-six), Essex (eighty-five), Suffolk (seventy-four) and Somerset (sixty-eight). In general the places where tokens were issued were most numerous in the counties stretching from Cornwall eastward to Kent, around London and then along the east coast as far as Yorkshire. They were thinner on the ground in the west Midlands and the counties bordering Wales (for example, Shropshire with twenty places, Cheshire with ten and Worcestershire with twenty-one). Even allowing for the adjustments necessary because of the different sizes of counties, it is not clear how much can safely be deduced from this sort of distribution. It may simply reflect a natural correlation between the number of places where tokens were issued and the density of population. On the other hand the distribution rather suggests some correlation between the number of places where tokens were issued and the general level of regional economic development in the middle of the seventeenth century. It could be argued that this correlation, if it exists, merely confirms what is known about economic development at this time, but not everyone would subscribe to the austere doctrine that statistics which merely confirm what we already know, or think we know, are unnecessary and irrelevant. More esoteric correlations between the issue of tokens and, say, the incidence of hearth tax could no doubt be made, and probably will be.

The 7,787 different tokens issued between 1649 and 1672 were not, of course, necessarily issued by shopkeepers. The problem is to isolate those that were so issued. For this purpose the tokens can be divided into four categories. The first consists of tokens on which the issuer is described as mercer, draper, grocer or other type of shopkeeper. Thus the Macclesfield tokens include one issued by 'Edward Wood Mercer in Macksfield in Chersheir', and the Ripon tokens include one issued by 'Lancelot Williamson in Rippon Grocer'.[61] The second category consists of tokens that have no occupational description, but bear the arms of one of the London livery companies, usually the Mercers', Drapers' or Grocers' Company. The use of the London companies' arms on provincial tokens is interesting, and may be some indication that the tokens were made in London. It may seem fanciful at first sight to assume that 'a demi-virgin, couped below the shoulders, issuing from clouds, crowned, hair dishevelled, all within an orle of clouds', denotes a mercer, and indeed in some bad specimens she is sometimes mistaken for the King's Head inn sign,[62] but there is no doubt that the provincial shopkeepers used the appropriate London arms on their tokens. Indeed it is quite common for a man to be described as a mercer on a token which bears the Mercers' arms. Where tokens bear a London company's arms which denote a retailer, I have counted them, along with those in the first category, as being issued by shopkeepers.

The third category is more ambiguous. It consists of tokens which bear a part of a London company's arms or which bear some device or symbol denoting occupation. Perhaps the most common symbols are the stick of candles and the man making candles which usually denote a chandler. The roll of tobacco is also common as are the pair of scales and the sugar loaf. It is clear from the evidence of the tokens themselves that a pair of scales could be the symbol for mercers, bakers, chandlers and grocers, and that the sugar loaf was used as a device by grocers, mercers, chandlers and drapers. I have assumed that tokens in this third category, whether based on parts of coats of arms or on symbols, may have been issued by shopkeepers and have therefore classified them separately as 'possibles'. This may err on the side of caution. The fourth category of tokens is rather a mixed bag. It includes the tokens issued by town authorities and tokens which give an occupation other than that of shopkeeper. for example carriers, clothiers, millers and dyers. It includes also a very large number of innkeepers, though some apparent inn signs on tokens may in fact be shop signs. Finally it includes the most difficult tokens of all, those which give no indication whatsoever of the issuer's occupation. That occupation can sometimes be discovered from local research using other sources, and where that has been done the issuer is often shown to have been a shopkeeper. Thus research into the token issuers at Oxford has added about a dozen shopkeepers to those issuers who could be classified as shopkeepers from the evidence of their tokens alone.[63] This work has only been done for certain places, and I have not made use of it in classifying the tokens. I have relied on the evidence of the tokens themselves as given in Williamson. This means that my figures of the number of shopkeepers, even if the 'possibles' are included, are an underestimate, and almost certainly a serious underestimate.

When these categories are applied to the tokens they show that tokens were issued by 2,151 shopkeepers (or 2,683 if the 'possibles' are included). These 2,151 shopkeepers were headed by the grocers (730) and the mercers (558), followed by chandlers (156), bakers (120), drapers (117), apothecaries (ninety-four), ironmongers (eight-three) and haberdashers (fifty-two). The remainder included shoemakers (thirty-four), butchers (twenty-six), merchant tailors (twenty-two),[64] fishmongers (thirteen), milliners (eleven), pewterers (eleven), booksellers (ten), saddlers (seven), stationers (five), and goldsmiths (four). Too much should not be made of these descriptions which, especially in the case of grocer, mercer, draper and haberdasher, could cover a fairly un-specialised shop. There are indeed tokens which imply this. John Beale of Faversham issued a token in 1649 on which he was described as a mercer, but the token bore the Mercers' arms on the obverse and the Grocers' arms on the reverse.[65] Similarly Richard Short of Wardington in Oxfordshire described himself as a mercer on his token which bore only the Grocers' arms.[66] The considerable number of chandlers who issued tokens is a reminder of a rather forgotten trade. Many were described as tallow chandlers, and their number would be greatly increased if the 'possibles' were added. They reflect the demand for candles which was very heavy, especially in the big households. Charles Howard of Naworth spent £11 16s 9d in buying candles at Brampton, Newcastle and Penrith between August 1648 and March 1649, and this despite the fact that he provided some of the tallow.[67] The numbers probably also reflect the fact that many chandlers had developed into more general shopkeepers. Thomas Allen of Brigstock in Northamptonshire described himself as a chandler on his token, but the token bore the Grocers' not the Tallow Chandlers' arms.[68]

Though the number of token-issuing shopkeepers is quite impressive, it is less significant than the number of places in which those tokens were issued. Shopkeepers issued tokens in 822 cities, towns and villages, and the number rises to 949 places if the 'possibles' are included. These 822 places were unevenly distributed. As might be expected their distribution corresponds roughly to the distribution of token issuers as a whole. Thus of the 822 places only twenty-two were in Wales and one in Monmouthshire; the northern counties were poorly represented with none in Cumberland, one each in Westmorland and Northumberland and three in Durham. As before, the county table was headed by Kent (sixty places), but now followed by Suffolk (forty-nine), Yorkshire (forty-one), Norfolk (thirty-eight), Lincolnshire (thirty-six), and Sussex (thirty-five). It is not clear whether this county distribution has any special significance or whether it is some index of regional economic development. Considering the nature of the evidence, such an index could more reasonably be based on the distribution of places where any tokens were issued rather than on places where shopkeepers' tokens were issued. The 822 places where shopkeepers' tokens were issued are obviously significant evidence for the distribution of shops. The number of places is roughly equal to the number of market towns in England and Wales in 1640. Many market towns, however, had no shopkeepers who issued tokens, and so many tokens were issued by shopkeepers whose shops were not in market towns. About 330 places which were not market towns had shopkeepers who issued tokens; the number rises to about 400 if the 'possibles' are included. These 330 places were found in all parts of the country, but they were most numerous in the counties of Kent, Suffolk, Sussex, Surrey and Norfolk. They were fairly numerous in Cambridgeshire, Derbyshire, Essex, Hampshire, Lincolnshire, Middlesex and Wiltshire. Again it is difficult to assess the significance of this distribution. It suggests the obvious and trite conclusion that, in general, shops outside market towns were more numerous in those counties where market towns were fewer in number and more scattered. At least it shows that, even if market day were a shopping day, in many places it was not necessary to go to market in order to shop.

The most interesting feature of the tokens is the evidence they provide of the existence of shops in so many small places, with or without markets, and of shops whose owners felt it was worthwhile to issue tokens. Thus to take Yorkshire as an example, it is more significant to find token-issuing shopkeepers at places like Gisburne, Middleham and Sedbergh than it is at places like York, Doncaster and Hull. Middleham had a market and an imposing castle, but neither explains why two grocers there, Lawrence Cave and Charles Todd, should have issued halfpenny tokens in 1666 and 1668 respectively.[69] Perhaps one copied the other, or perhaps they both succumbed to the persuasions of the token makers or their agents. It would be wrong to assume that these shopkeeper tokens provide a complete picture of the distribution of shops in this period. Obviously many shopkeepers did not issue tokens, and others may have issued tokens of which no specimen has survived. The chief value of the tokens in the history of retail trade is to show how widespread shops were and to provide evidence, often unique evidence, of the existence of shops in small places. The tokens may provide the nearest thing that we can get to a directory of shopkeepers before the appearance of the national directories in the 1780s. Indeed the tokens have one advantage over the directories, for they reveal the existence of shops in places too small to be included in the earlier directories.

It is plainly possible to get some idea of the type and distribution of provincial shops in the seventeenth century, but it is more difficult to get material for those case studies which would put some flesh on the skeleton. Business records of shopkeepers do not seem to have survived, and shopkeepers themselves rarely left any personal account of their life and work. Only two such personal accounts seem to have come down to us; they are the diary of Roger Lowe and the autobiography of William Stout. Both are worth some consideration for their contribution to an understanding of retail trade.

Roger Lowe's diary covers, very unsystematically, the years from 1663 to March 1674, but there is only a single entry after March 1669.[70] When the diary opens Lowe was an apprentice in charge of a shop at Ashton-in-Makerfield in Lancashire; his master was a shopkeeper at Leigh, some five miles east of Ashton.

Lowe was an orphan, but nothing is known of his parents or of his early background. He could read, write and do accounts, and certainly knew some Latin. These skills made him in great demand as a writer of letters for the illiterate and as an inditer of bonds and wills. For these services he was paid in cash or ale, but he was not always allowed to keep the cash. In April 1663 his master took £3 from Lowe that he 'had gotten with writeinge', to his 'great griefe'; this was no doubt on the grounds that an apprentice's earnings on the side belonged to his master. Within a fortnight Lowe was reconciled by the present of 'a suite of clothes' from his master, 'which did much comfort me'.[71] Lowe lived, or rather slept, at the shop in Ashton, but it was no lonely bachelor life. There was some decorous courting, much eating out at friends' houses, occasional fishing, hunting, horse racing (on a borrowed horse), bowling (for money) and a great deal of drinking in ale houses. As a presbyterian Lowe felt deep remorse for some of these activities. He tried to justify the drinking on the grounds that it was necessary for his trade. When he was 'envited to goe to Gawther Taylor's to drinke', he accepted because Taylor's wife 'bought her comodities of me, and she said if I would not come, then farewell'. When 'old Mr. Woods came to shoppe' and warned Lowe about his drinking, 'I tolde hime I could not trade if att some times I did not spend 2d'.[72] In a country place, where custom can be mutual, such excuses have some justification, But Lowe seems to have spent almost as much time in the ale house as in the shop. His diary does not suggest that application to business which is sometimes seen as characteristic of the nonconformist; nor does his way of life conform to the puritan stereotype. Even allowing for the apprentice's normal discontent with his 'servitude', it is difficult to believe that Lowe found shopkeeping an absorbing pursuit, which may be one reason why he tells us so little about it.

Lowe would probably have described himself as a mercer, but there is little evidence of what he sold in the shop at Ashton. Most of the stock was brought from his master's shop at Leigh; it included cloth and candles, but it was usually simply described as commodities or goods. Lowe himself was allowed to buy goods, some of which were for the Leigh shop. He bought candles and currants at Warrington,[73] 'twist for coates' at Wigan,[74] scythe stones and scythes,[75] honey and wax[76] and hour-glasses. The hour-glasses he bought from 'Henry Feildinge, an hower glasse maker' for 10s a dozen 'and sold them after 12',[77] which was his only recorded profit margin. As Lowe had to spend time going round collecting debts, it seems clear that he sold some goods on credit. Naturally as a mere apprentice acting as manager, Lowe had to settle accounts with his master. On these occasions John Chadocke, another apprentice, 'came from Leigh to cast up shop', and Lowe, so full of apprehension that he 'slept litle' the previous night, went to Leigh for the reckoning.[78] In February 1664 Lowe 'cast up debt bookes and see how I stood with my Master' and found that he had received from his master goods to the value of £148 8s 9d in the past year, of which he had sold £135 5s 1d worth.[79] At the accounting in May it was found that he had 'profited' his master £21 1s 5d, which was regarded as satisfactory.[80] The next accounting was in November 1665 when Lowe 'was chargd with £201' and 'had profited £48'.[81] This would appear to mean that in the eighteen months between the two reckonings, Lowe had received goods to the value of £201 and had made a profit of £48 or 24 per cent.

This was the last of the accounting days for at that time Lowe was released from his apprenticeship and allowed to take over the shop and stock at Ashton. He was given time to pay his master for the stock and indeed received further goods from him. As an independent shopkeeper Lowe was a more typical retailer than he had been as an apprentice and manager. This direct transition from apprentice to independent shopkeeper seems to have been common, although it allowed for no intervening stage as a journeyman during which capital might be accumulated. Lowe himself was conscious of his lack of capital and was 'sadly troubled for fear of miscaryinge'.[82] There was only one solution and that was to obtain goods on credit. A Yorkshireman supplied Lowe with cloth at three months' credit, and other goods were bought in Warrington 'upon trust'.[83] Naturally Lowe had to do much more buying than before when most of his stock had been provided from Leigh. He bought goods at Liverpool and Warrington and at Chester Fair, where he dealt with Bristol and London merchants.[84] Some at least of these goods he managed to pay for, but the debt to his former master for the stock taken over was more difficult to repay. Lowe had to provide two sureties for its repayment, one of whom ran away.[88] Two years after gaining his independence, Lowe gave up the struggle to maintain it. In October 1667 he quitted himself 'of all shop effaires in Ashton and resigned them over to Thomas Hamond' and engaged himself 'in Thomas Peake's service'. Peake was a Warrington shopkeeper whom Lowe agreed to serve for three years for £20. It was an unfortunate choice; Mrs Peake was 'of such a pestilentiall nature' that Lowe was 'weary in a few weekes'.[86] How long he remained with Peake is uncertain; he married in March 1668, but after that there are less than a dozen entries in the diary and they tell little of his movements. There is no doubt that Lowe returned to live at Ashton where he combined shopkeeping with some farming. When he died in 1679 he was described as a husbandman of Ashton. His probate inventory, which valued his personal estate at £60 6s 4d, shows that he owned two milk cows worth £6 and 'goods beinge in the shop' worth £29 3s. The bedstead and bedding 'in the roome over the shop' imply that Lowe lived on the shop premises; the absence of agricultural implements or utensils, except for a churn, suggests that he was more of a shopkeeper than farmer,[87] though even as an apprentice he had bought a heifer in calf for 39s.[88] Perhaps when Lowe resumed shopkeeping he sold his own milk or butter.

Lowe was a village shopkeeper; as such he worked in a rural society which seems to have been reasonably tolerant and easygoing. Neither he nor his friends and neighbours give the impression that they regarded time as money or thought that life was a ceaseless competition for material gain. It was a society with its own unspoken conventions to which Lowe conformed. These demanded a certain conviviality and neighbourliness among the living and a certain respect to the dead. Lowe was a great attender at funerals, but it would be wrong to think of this as a mere pretext for getting away from the shop; the dead may have been a neighbour or customer, and convention demanded the last respects in either case. Lowe combined an intensity of religious feeling with a curious casualness in his attitude to his work and his social life. That casualness may have derived simply from his own nature, but it may equally well have reflected a rural attitude towards the things of this world. It was certainly very different from the more intense and urbanised atmosphere in which Stout lived and worked.

William Stout was born in 1665, the son of a yeoman of Bolton

Holmes, near Bolton-le-Sands, in north Lancashire.[89] His father died when Stout was sixteen, leaving him about £150 in land and money, and very soon after the boy was apprenticed to Henry Coward, a Quaker grocer and ironmonger of Lancaster. The premium was £20, presumably paid out of Stout's inheritance.[90] As an apprentice Stout slept in the shop and worked there 'with the windows open' until nine in the evening and 'with the windows shut and the dore open until ten o'clock'. Even that might not be the end of the day's work for he was 'frequently caled up at altimes of the night to serve customers'. Stout spent much of his time 'in making up goods for the market day' as sugar, tobacco, nails 'and particularly prunes'. The shop sold about a hundredweight of prunes a week in summer; they were bought at 8s to 9s cwt, and sold at 4d for 3 lb. This suggests a retail margin of about 33 per cent, which was much less than on the tobacco bought at 2d lb and 'retailed at 6d'. For a time Coward also had a shop at Bolton-le-Sands which Stout managed 'two days weekly', but the shop did not answer expectations and was abandoned.[91] Had it been retained Stout might have completed his apprenticeship as an apprentice manager as Lowe did. There is no doubt that Stout was a more industrious apprentice than Lowe had been. When 'out of nessesary business' in the shop, he spent his time in 'reading; or improving my selfe in arethmatick, survighing or other mathamatikall sciences' and 'never thought the time long to be out of my apprintishipe as too many youths are'.[92] Moreover under the influence and example of his master he was embracing the Quaker faith.

Stout ended his seven-year apprenticeship in 1688 when he rented a shop in Lancaster for £5 per annum. Though he took a small room off the shop 'for a bed, table and a smal light' and slept there, he boarded with a neighbour for £5 per annum 'victuals and washing'. Like most beginners in trade Stout was faced with the problem of acquiring the necessary capital for buying stock. In this he was better placed than many, for he was able to use the £119 10s which remained of his father's legacy and to borrow £10 from his sister which he 'kept many years'. He borrowed £12 from an unnamed lender, but this he repaid in a year. Taking £120 of this money he set out for London on a horse borrowed from his brother Josias and in company with other Lancaster shopkeepers. They arrived in the capital five days later, which implies long days in the saddle, and lodged at the Swan with Two Necks in Lad Lane where, according to John Taylor, the Manchester carriers lodged. Stout bought goods to the value of £200 or upwards and paid about half in ready money, 'as was then usual to do by any young man beginning trade'. The goods were sent to Lancaster by sea while Stout returned home via Sheffield where he spent some £20 in 'Sheffeild and Birmingham manufactories'. The shop was open in time for the Midsummer Fair when Stout had 'good encouragement' in his trade. His sister Ellen came to help during the fair and on market days and indeed looked after both the shop and her brother when Stout was ill during the autumn of 1688.[93] By 1689, according to Stout, the war with France was raising the price of French prunes and resin and was disrupting the sea passage between London and Lancaster, so that there was 'now no carriage from London but by land' which cost 3s to 5s cwt to Standish and 1s 6d cwt from Standish to Lancaster. It is doubtful if the effects of war were being felt so soon and, if they were, how far they affected Stout's trade. His main difficulty arose from being 'too forward in trusting and too backward in caling, as is too frequent with young tradesmen'. In other words, he had sold too much on credit and had been too slow in getting in the debts. This left him short of capital, and he borrowed £40 upon bond, of which £30 was used to buy more goods in Sheffield. At the end of his first year's trading in May 1689 Stout found that he had sold goods 'for ready money about £450 and upon credit about £150' and that he 'had gained this year about fifty pounds beside shop rent and bording'.[94]

Stout had made a good start and he now began to acquire some of the marks of the prospering shopkeeper. In 1690 he bought a horse instead of borrowing one and took an apprentice, John Troughton, whose mother provided a premium of £20 and the boy's clothes. Stout provided maintenance, which meant that Troughton slept at the shop but boarded out with his master. This arrangement presumably ended the following year when Stout rented more rooms (a great parlour, cellar and three bedrooms) and set up housekeeping with his sister Ellen as housekeeper.[95] Meanwhile the shop quietly prospered, though there are few details of the trade. Around 1692 a quarter of the sales was of tobacco; sugar, bought at Liverpool, was also sold and cheese, bought at Preston Fair, was in great demand as a funeral meat. As much as 30 to 100 lb of cheese might be sold for a single funeral according to the 'ability' of the deceased.[96] Ironmongery was rarely mentioned, but the purchase of goods at Sheffield shows that it was still sold. All these things contributed to a steady profit despite bad debts. In 1697 when Stout 'inspected my books', he found that in nine years' trading he had lost £220 through 248 insolvent debtors. In spite of these losses, his 'clear estate was eleven hundred and upwards' so that his 'improvement in nine years was above one hundred pounds a year, one year with another'. This calculation was made because Stout had decided to give up retail trading. In 1697 his apprentice, John Troughton, completed his apprenticeship, and Stout handed over the shop to him on payment of £187 for the stock and equipment of scales, boxes and chests. This was to be paid 'at six, twelve and eighteen months', which was duly performed.[97]

On his retirement from shopkeeping Stout took to shipowning and foreign trade, but with less success than he had had in retailing. Even so, his return to the inland trade was accidental. On the death of his friend and neighbour, Augustin Greenwood, a wholesale grocer, in 1701, Stout valued the stock and, on the failure of a would-be purchaser to give security, himself bought it. Thus he found himself 'selling grocery goods by whole sale to country shopkeepers'.[98] Three years later his former apprentice, Troughton, failed, and Stout bought his stock and set up shop again. He also took over Troughton's apprentice, John Hull, who had two years to serve, and got a premium of £30 for the two years.[99] Stout himself, combining wholesale and retail trade and foreign ventures, modestly prospered.

It would be rash to generalise too much from the evidence presented by Lowe and Stout, but their works, and especially Stout's, do suggest some general features of shopkeeping at this time. They show that the normal entry into shopkeeping was by apprenticeship and that apprentices had usually received some 'secondary' education. Stout attended Heversham Grammar School and then followed its headmaster, Thomas Lodge, to Lancaster Grammar School. After his father's death, Stout had a three weeks' cramming course in writing and arithmetic with a scrivener before entering his apprenticeship.[100] Lowe was sufficiently well educated not only to act as a sort of freelance scrivener but to be given the task of teaching his master's son, 'litle Thomas', a task which grieved him 'very sore'.[101] This need for at least a basic education in the three Rs may have meant that these boys were rather older when they were apprenticed than was the case in manual crafts. It is clear that apprenticeship involved a premium which varied with the repute and experience of the master. Stout received £20 with his first apprentice in 1690 and £35 with John Good in 1714.[102] For this the master had to provide training, board and lodgings and sometimes clothes for the apprentice, though in Lancaster it was not unusual for the boy's father to provide the clothes. In return the apprentice served his master, and was obviously given considerable responsibility. Lowe managed the Ashton shop and Stout managed his master's shop at Bolton-le-Sands for a time. Lowe's fellow apprentice, John Chadocke, did the annual stocktaking at Ashton. Apprentices must in fact have acted as shop assistants during their apprenticeship. Stout had the help of his sister Ellen during busy periods in the shop, but when he wanted more continuous assistance he took an apprentice and then had 'more time to divert my selfe'.[103] Some assistance was almost essential with shops open for long hours of the day and night, and the shopkeeper needing to travel around to buy his stock. Such assistance seems rarely to have taken the form of employing a journeyman. It is true that Lowe acted as a journeyman in Peake's shop, but there is no mention of journeymen in Stout.

When the apprentice had completed his apprenticeship he became, according to Stout's evidence, a shopkeeper without any intervening period as a journeyman assistant. This may have reflected, not so much the lack of openings for journeymen, as the social and economic position of the apprentice's father, who regarded it as perfectly respectable for his son to be an apprentice, but less respectable for him to be a journeyman. After all a man did not pay a premium to make his son into a shop assistant but to make him into a shopkeeper. Apprentices seem to have come from families where the father was prepared not only to pay a substantial premium for apprenticeship but also to provide the capital necessary for setting the boy up as a shopkeeper as soon as his apprenticeship was completed. Capital was essential for setting up in business as a shopkeeper. It was almost wholly circulating capital, for the shop could be rented and the fittings made cheaply by the local joiner. Thus Stout rented his first shop for £5 per annum and 'employed a joyner to make chests and draw boxes to fitt the shop'.[104] Inventories show that these shopfittings need not be expensive. Joseph Clarke, a grocer and draper of Roxwell in Essex who died in 1692, had 'boxes, shelves, scales and weights' in his shop which were valued at £2.[105] The need for circulating capital could be reduced by buying goods on credit or partly on credit. Lowe clearly did this and so did Stout in his early days as a shopkeeper. But credit worked both ways, for the shopkeeper gave credit to his customers. Lowe spent much time in collecting debts, and a quarter of Stout's early sales were on credit, which compelled him to further borrowing when the debts were slow to come in.

Though capital was necessary for stocking a shop, it provided no guarantee of success for the shopkeeper. In 1697 Stout's first apprentice, John Troughton, took over his master's stock in trade for £187, which he paid for in eighteen months, but by 1704 he was bankrupt with debts of above £1,200 and assets of £430. Troughton's apprentice, John Hull, completed his apprenticeship under Stout and was provided with 'a suficient stock to begin trade' by his father, the vicar of Walton near Preston. Hull 'was not diligent in his busines' and 'overrun his creddit in a few years and broke'.[106] Even Stout's nephew William went bankrupt, though he had been apprenticed to his uncle who amply provided him with stock and money to set up shopkeeping.[107] No doubt Stout laid stronger emphasis on those who failed in business than on those who succeeded. To him such failures were the result of moral shortcomings: inattention to business, too much drinking, too much high living. Perhaps there was a greater element of bad luck in some of these failures than Stout would admit, but his depressing list of bankrupts is a useful reminder of the risks involved in retail trade. Whether the risks were greater in Lancaster than elsewhere cannot be determined. In smaller places the competition may have been less keen and the failures proportionately less numerous. It is difficult to imagine Roger Lowe surviving even as a manager apprentice in Lancaster; he would certainly not have met with Stout's approval.

The picture presented by the activities of Lowe and Stout does not suggest any radical change in the general pattern of retail trade in the seventeenth century. Even if the general pattern were maintained, there may have been some changes of detail. In the early eighteenth century Nicholas Blundell of Little Crosby, some six miles north of Liverpool, was getting his goods from the usual sources tapped by the minor gentry. He bought cloth from pedlars, John Steward and his wife, to whom he sold rabbit skins, and bought 'a periwig of horse hair from a woman that came past my gates'.[108] Cloth, gloves, starch, capers and other goods were got at Chester Fair.[109] Little was bought in London except occasional articles of clothing and coffee. The coffee at 6s and 6s 8d lb was adulterated, for Blundell had to pick stones out of it.[110] The main shopping centre was clearly Liverpool where Blundell bought groceries, wine, cloth, clover seeds, physic and pottery,[111] and where he sold some of his farm and garden produce. This was all rather reminiscent of the Shuttleworths a century earlier, but there was one difference that may have been significant. Blundell was much less dependent on buying in London than the Shuttleworths had been. Some of the goods he bought in Liverpool may have come from London, as many of Stout's goods did, but if so they came as part of the stock of a Liverpool shopkeeper who was cutting in between the London retailer and the provincial consumer. There may have been more reliance on local shops, but there is little evidence that such shops were becoming more specialised in the London manner. They absorbed new products like tobacco and tobacco pipes, tea and coffee; Blundell for example got coffee from his Liverpool grocer as well as from London.[112] Drapers added clothes to their cloth. In 1708 Blundell's wife could buy a 'callico sute' in Preston,[113] and in the same year John Butler, a woollen draper of King's Lynn, had a considerable stock of ready made clothes. He sold 'cheskwered shirts', 'yellow westcoates', 'lades coates', 'chelldren frocks', 'menes britches' and 'menes dubll bristed coates', vests and stuff gowns.[114] Such items do not seem to appear in the inventories of an earlier period.

If the shops did not get more specialised, the shopkeepers may have done so in the sense of losing their agricultural interests. Roger Lowe had some interest in farming, as his inventory shows, but Stout, who came of farming stock, had no such interest. His master, Henry Coward, kept horses and a cow, and a man to look after them, but Coward pretended 'skill in horses', which was one of the things that 'drew him from his nessesary business' and helped to ruin him.[115] Shopkeepers kept horses and could ride them, but modern shopkeepers often keep motor vans and can drive them, which does not mean that they should be classified as motor mechanics. Stout's picture of the Lancaster shopkeepers suggests that they were urbanised and had lost any contact with the land, except perhaps as an investment. The failures did not seek a new life on the land; they wandered off or went mad or got a Waiter's place in the Customs.[116] The evidence of probate inventories also suggests that the combination of shopkeeping and farming was not very common. At Lichfield an apothecary who died in 1655 kept a cow and a pig, but other shopkeepers there had either no agricultural stock or simply kept pigs.[117] The same was true of a small place like Petworth where a few tradesmen kept a horse and a very few a pig.[118] No doubt such back-yard farming survived elsewhere, but it is of no great significance.

Though provincial shops may not have become more specialised in the seventeenth century, it is very probable that their numbers had increased. In 1681 it was alleged 'that which hath been the bane almost of all trades is the too great number of shopkeepers in this kingdom'. Shopkeeping had increased because of the decline of other trades, especially the cloth trade, and because it was 'an easy life' which attracted 'husbandmen, labourers, and artificers, who have left off their working trades, and turned shopkeepers'. Previously shopkeeping had been 'both a convenient and easy way for the gentry, clergy, and commonalty of this kingdom to provide for their younger sons'. They had done this through apprenticeship which cost them 'in a country market town not less than fifty or sixty pounds'. Thus the shopkeeping trade had been bought 'with the parent's money, and the son's servitude', and it should be confined to those 'made free of the same'. Now, however, apprenticeship had declined and 'in every country village where is (it may be) not above ten houses, there is a shopkeeper, and one that never served any apprenticeship to any shopkeeping trade whatsoever'. Moreover many such village shopkeepers did not deal only in 'pins or such small wares', but 'in as many substantial commodities as any do that live in cities and market towns'. This had caused the depopulation and impoverishment of cities and market towns by intercepting 'a very great part of the trade from coming to them'. It had interrupted the normal exchange between town and country, which was based on country people selling their produce in the market town and buying from shops there. The tradesmen in cities and market towns could no longer 'buy the farmers' commodities, and help them constantly to money for them, if they should always go home, and lay out little or no part thereof again with them'.[119]

Not all this special pleading should be taken at its face value. Apprenticeship still seems to have been the normal way of entry into shopkeeping, and it would be difficult to prove that cities and towns were becoming impoverished, and still more difficult to prove that such impoverishment was the result of competition from village shops. On the other hand the emphasis on the growth in the number of shops may be justified, even if it is difficult to prove statistically. Other evidence, whether trade tokens, inventories or travellers' accounts, rather suggests such a growth. So too does Gregory King's estimate of forty thousand families of shopkeepers in 1688. They were said to have a yearly income of £45 per family,[120] which was £15 less than Stout's income at that time.

There could be many reasons for an increase in the number of provincial shops in this period. It might be caused by a decline in other forms of retailing. More shops would be necessary if markets were becoming less important or pedlars less numerous, but there is no evidence at all of this. It could arise from the growth of population with a corresponding increase in the size of towns and villages. Such a growth and increase occurred, though their causes and extent remain uncertain. It was not, however, simply an increase in numbers that mattered, but the demand for goods generated by that increase. Assuming that people as a whole were not becoming worse off, the mere increase in numbers would produce increased demand. That demand would be greater still if at least a section of the community were improving its standard of living and buying more goods as part of that improvement. Some evidence suggests that this was happening. Not much can be learned about the increase in home production, except perhaps in coal and cloth, but rising imports reflected increased demand even when due allowance is made for re-exports. Retained imports of tobacco, wine and spirits, calico, linen and silk, sugar and other groceries increased after the Restoration more than the rise in population.[121] This import trade was still heavily concentrated on London, but that did not mean that the goods were necessarily consumed in the capital. London retained its function as a centre for the distribution of imported goods to the provinces. In the year ending at Christmas 1628 London shipped coastwise 352 cargoes to some fifty provincial ports. By the year ending at Christmas 1683 the number of cargoes had risen to 1001; they went to some sixty-six provincial ports, and 545 cargoes included tobacco and 488 included grocery wares amounting to 3,000 tons.[122] These goods, and others, entered into the retail trade of the ports and their hinterlands.

This rising demand is reflected in household inventories with their increasing quantities of linen, plate and furnishings of all kinds. It is reflected, too, in the contents of shops with their stocks of expensive cloths and trimmings and of their rather expensive groceries. No doubt much of this demand came from the middle ranks of society, both rural and urban, but the effect of their increasing opulence on the nature and distribution of shops remains uncertain. It has been said that after 1600 'in virtually every county the smaller towns tended to lose ground to the larger as shopping and marketing centres'.[123] This might happen if there were an increasing demand for the type of goods that shops in villages or small market towns did not or could not stock, but there seems little evidence of this in the seventeenth century. Whether or not the larger towns absorbed the trade and annexed the hinterland of smaller towns,[124] they certainly generated their own demand through rising population and changing social habits. Thus Norwich's population rose from perhaps twelve thousand to thirty thousand in the seventeenth century, and the city developed a winter 'season' which 'catered for the middle rank gentry, the country clergy and prosperous farmers'.[125] The 'season' of the county capitals could hardly have developed if the capitals had not already possessed an 'urban gentry', which often had county connections and was reinforced by the growing number of professional men and by members of the commercial patriciate.[126] Such changes in the size and social stratification of the larger towns must have affected both the number and nature of urban shops, but little is known of this or indeed of the social stratification itself. In the prevailing state of ignorance, it is safest to conclude with a general observation. The present interest in demand as a factor in economic growth should include an interest in what people actually bought and where they bought it.

Notes

1 *Shuttleworth accounts*, ii. 252.

2 *Ibid.*, i. 197, 212, ii. 242, 250.

3 G. Ornsby, ed., *Selections from the household books of Lord William Howard of Naworth Castle*, Surtees Soc., lxviii (1877), 25–6, 304.

4 *Ibid.*, 94, 160, 196, 329.

5 *Ibid.*, 43, 327.

6 A. M. C. Forster, ed., *Selections from the Disbursements Book (1691–1709) of Sir Thomas Haggerston, Bart.*, Surtees Soc., clxxx (1969), 4, 19, 26, 41, 49.

7 H. Best, *Rural economy in Yorkshire in 1641*, ed. C. B. Robinson, Surtees Soc., xxxiii (1857), pp. 112–13.

8 *Infra*. pp. 91, 94.

9 *H.M.C. Portland*, ii. 269.

10 C. Morris, ed., *The journeys of Celia Fiennes*, pp. 147–8.

11 *Ibid.*, pp. 96, 130, 133–4; C. W. Chalklin, *Seventeenth-century Kent*, pp. 156–8.

12 1 Jas. I, c. 7.

13 G. H. Kenyon, 'Kirdford inventories, 1611 to 1776', *Sussex Arch. Collections*, xciii (1955), 135–6.

14 G. Ornsby, ed., *op. cit.*, p. 94.

15 N. Penny, ed., *The household account book of Sarah Fell of Swarthmoor Hall*, pp. 30, 63, 519.

16 J. R. Magrath, ed., *The Flemings in Oxford*, i (Oxford Historical Society, xliv, 1913), 421, 481, 496.

17 A. M. C. Forster, ed., *op. cit.*, pp. 7, 10, 12, 26, 30, 33, 35.

18 *Journals of the House of Commons*, xi. 3, 14, 61, 108, 146, 338, 426; J. Thirsk and J. P. Cooper, eds., *Seventeenth-century economic documents*, pp. 417–21.

19 8/9 Wm. III, c. 25.

20 Lowe, pp. 27, 67.

21 H. Best, *op. cit.*, p. 106.

22 H. Horwitz, ed., *The parliamentary diary of Narcissus Luttrell 1691–1693*, p. 324.

23 D. M. Woodward, 'The Chester leather industry, 1558–1625', *Trans. Historic Soc. of Lancs. and Cheshire*, 119 (1967), p. 76.

24 G. H. Kenyon, 'Petworth town and trades, 1610–1760', *Sussex Arch. Collections*, xcvi (1958), 75.

25 L. B. and M. W. Barley, 'Lincolnshire craftsmen in the

sixteenth and seventeenth centuries', *Lincolnshire Historian*, ii (1959), 10.

[26] W. B. Stephens, ed., *History of Congleton*, p. 54.

[27] P. R. Mounfield, *The footwear industry in the East Midlands*, p. 396.

[28] D. G. Vaisey, ed., *Probate inventories of Lichfield and district 1568–1680*, Staffordshire Record Soc. (1969), pp. 130–1, 151–2.

[29] F. C. Morgan, 'Inventories of a Hereford saddler's shop in the years 1692 and 1696', *Trans. Woolhope Naturalists' Field Club*, xxxi (1942–5), 253–68.

[30] L. B. and M. W. Barley, 'Lincolnshire shopkeepers in the sixteenth and seventeenth centuries', *Lincolnshire Historian*, ii (1962), 10–11.

[31] C. Morris, ed., *op. cit.*, pp. 170, 210–11.

[32] 'The Sankeys, mercers, of Ormskirk,' L.R.O. *Report* for 1965, pp. 37–45.

[33] J. J. Bagley, 'Matthew Markland, a Wigan mercer', *Trans. Lancs. and Cheshire Arch. Soc.*, lxviii (1958), 45–66.

[34] D. G. Vaisey, 'A Charlbury mercer's shop', *Oxoniensia*, xxxi (1968), 107–116.

[35] G. C. Boon, *Welsh tokens of the seventeenth century*, pp. 43–75.

[36] D. G. Vaisey, ed., *Probate inventories of Lichfield and district 1568–1680*, pp. 126–8.

[37] F. W. Steer, ed., *Farm and cottage inventories of mid-Essex 1635–1749*, pp. 169–70.

[38] Inventory in L.R.O.

[39] Inventory in L.R.O.

[40] The accounts are written on the blank pages in the first parish register of Nantwich Parish Church. There is a xerox copy of them in the Cheshire Record Office, Chester.

[41] E. Garton, *Nantwich Saxon to Puritan*, pp. 99–100.

[42] Ten of the hats seem to have been returned to Tench.

[43] *Journals of the House of Commons*, i. 469–70.

[44] N. J. Williams, ed., *Tradesmen in Early Stuart Wiltshire*, Wilts. Arch. and Natural History Soc., Records Branch, xv (1960), p. xxi.

[45] R. Hughey, ed., *The correspondence of Lady Katherine Paston, 1603–1627*, Norfolk Record Soc., xiv (1941), 71.

[46] Williams, *op. cit.*, p. xxi.

[47] M. W. Beresford, 'The beginning of retail tobacco licences, 1632–1641', *Yorkshire Bulletin of Economic and Social Research*, vii (1955), 128–43.

[48] Mather of Lowick MSS., DD LK/14/4 (L.R.O.).

[49] The dates are often given as 1648 to 1672, but no tokens seem to have been issued before 1649 new style.

[50] I have used the 1967 reprint in three volumes (continuous pagination).

[51] See the Bibliography in J. L. Wetton, *Seventeenth century tradesmens' tokens*, Minerva Numismatic Handbooks, v (1969).

[52] E. Thurlow Leeds, 'Oxford tradesmens' tokens', in *Surveys and Tokens*, ed. H. E. Salter, Oxford Historical Society, lxxv (1923), 355–453.

[53] Wetton, *op. cit.*, p. 24.

[54] Williamson, i. p. xxi.

[55] G. C. Boon, *Welsh tokens of the seventeenth century*, pp. 26–7.

[56] E. Thurlow Leeds, *op. cit.*, p. 361.

[57] M. Weinstock, *Studies in Dorset history*, pp. 52–62.

[58] Williamson, iii. 1260.

[59] *Ibid.*, iii. 1429.

[60] London had 3,543 and Southwark 501 tokens.

[61] Williamson, i. 90, iii. 1336.

[62] Wetton, *op. cit.*, p. 22.

[63] E. Thurlow Leeds, *op. cit.*, pp. 378–453.

[64] There is some doubt whether these should be included as shopkeepers.

[65] Williamson, i. 365.

[66] *Ibid.*, ii. 935.

[67] C. R. Hudleston, ed., *Naworth estate and household accounts 1648–1660*, Surtees Soc., clxviii (1953), 42, 50.

[68] Williamson, ii. 887.

[69] Williamson, iii. 1330.

[70] Lowe, *passim*. There is an excellent study of Lowe in R. C. Latham, 'Roger Lowe, shopkeeper and nonconformist', *History*, n.s., xxvi (1941), 19–35. See also W. Notestein, *English folk*, pp. 217–43.

[71] Lowe, pp. 19–20.

[72] *Ibid.*, pp. 53, 59.

73 *Ibid.*, pp. 66, 93.
74 *Ibid.*, p. 73.
75 *Ibid.*, pp. 63, 67.
76 *Ibid.*, p. 69.
77 *Ibid.*, p. 60.
78 *Ibid.*, p. 60.
79 *Ibid.*, p. 52.
80 *Ibid.*, p. 61.
81 *Ibid.*, p. 93.
82 *Ibid.*, p. 93.
83 *Ibid.*
84 *Ibid.*, pp. 99–100, 104, 112, 118.
85 *Ibid.*, pp. 108, 111.
86 *Ibid.*, pp. 118–19.
87 *Ibid.*, pp. 133–4.
88 *Ibid.*, p. 81.
89 Stout, p. 67. It should be noted that some of the dates in the early part of the autobiography are inaccurate.
90 *Ibid.*, pp. 72–4.
91 *Ibid.*, pp. 79–80.
92 *Ibid.*, pp. 80–1, 88.
93 *Ibid.*, pp. 89–91.
94 *Ibid.*, pp. 95–6.
95 *Ibid.*, pp. 97–9, 102.
96 *Ibid.*, pp. 106–7.
97 *Ibid.*, pp. 118–20.
98 *Ibid.*, pp. 132, 148.
99 *Ibid.*, p. 150.
100 *Ibid.*, pp. 71–2, 74.
101 Lowe, p. 37.
102 Stout, p. 172. There is much information on apprenticeship premiums after 1710 when they were taxed (8 Anne, c. 5 sec. 40).
103 Stout, p. 99.
104 *Ibid.*, p. 89.
105 F. W. Steer, *op. cit.*, p. 213.
106 Stout, pp. 149–50.
107 *Ibid.*, pp. 200, 221.
108 F. Tyrer and J. J. Bagley, eds., *The Great Diurnal of Nicholas Blundell*, i, Record Soc. of Lancs, and Cheshire, 110 (1968),

pp. 20, 31, 87.

[109] *Ibid.*, i. 143 n. 260 n.

[110] *Ibid.*, i. 284, 310.

[111] *Ibid.*, i. 140, 210, 213, 228, 268.

[112] *Ibid.*, i. 140.

[113] *Ibid.*, i. 177.

[114] V. Parker, *The making of King's Lynn*, pp. 187–8.

[115] Stout, pp. 81, 121.

[116] *Ibid.*, pp. 100, 150.

[117] D. G. Vaisey, ed., *Probate inventories of Lichfield and district 1568–1680*, pp. 99–102, 118–20, 130–1.

[118] G. H. Kenyon, 'Petworth town and trades', pt. I, *Sussex Arch. Collections*, xcvi (1958), 36.

[119] J. Thirsk and J. P. Cooper, eds., *Seventeenth-century economic documents*, pp. 394–400.

[120] *Ibid.*, pp. 780–1.

[121] R. Davis, 'English foreign trade, 1660–1700' in W. E. Minchinton, ed., *The growth of English overseas trade in the seventeenth and eighteenth centuries*, pp. 78–98.

[122] T. S. Willan, *The English coasting trade, 1600–1750*, pp. 143–4, 203–5.

[123] A. Everitt, ed., *Perspectives in English urban history*, p. 216.

[124] *Ibid.*

[125] P. Clark and P. Slack, eds., *Crisis and order in English towns 1500–1700*, pp. 263, 291.

[126] A. Everitt, *op. cit.*, pp. 7–10.

IV A PROVINCIAL FIRM OF WHOLESALERS

The English economy during the Civil Wars and the Commonwealth has not been greatly studied.[1] Indeed some aspects of the economy, such as foreign trade, can hardly be studied with the detail possible before 1640 and after 1660, because of the lack of sources. This is true of the trade, either coastwise or foreign, of individual ports. Similarly the abolition of the prerogative courts removed one source of evidence which is often valuable for internal trade. Thus less is known of some branches of the economy than hitherto, and this loss is not made good by the great series of parliamentary surveys of crown and church lands, by the records of the sale of such lands and by the details of delinquents' estates. These reveal much about landholding, the land market and individual wealth, but on these topics a good deal is usually discoverable from other sources. The unsolved problem is what effects the wars and their aftermath had on the economy. Did they affect industrial output or disrupt established lines of trade? Such questions will have to be studied locally before any national conclusions can be drawn. Here it is proposed only to look at the activities of a firm of Lancashire cloth merchants which was sending cloth to the London market during the years 1644–51. This study is made possible by the chance survival of the accounts of a Rochdale partnership of cloth merchants for those years.[2] Rochdale was a centre of cloth production in the woollen cloth area of east Lancashire. By the mid seventeenth century it was the most important centre in that region, and its cloth had long found an outlet in the London market. It was in that London trade that the Rodes family partnership engaged.[3]

The composition of the partnership is not quite clear. It certainly included Abraham Rodes and his son John. The accounts of the partnership are in the names of these two men, but it is possible that another son, Abel, was also a partner. There are references in 1645 to a sum of money being 'reckned on his [Abel's] portyon', and in 1649 John Rodes wrote at the end of the year's account, '£500 of stocke in the London booke and in Rachdall booke belones to mee with the 3rd. parte of proffett of cloth this yeere', which suggests a partnership of three, though it is possible that Abraham had the other two parts. Abel, whether partner or not, seems to have worked in the Midlands, probably at Leicester, where he may have been engaged in the wool trade. Another son, Samuel, is mentioned in the accounts. He seems to have lived in London, but he was clearly not a member of the partnership. This was not one of those cases where a member of the family acted as the London representative of the firm.[4] Abraham and John Rodes worked in Rochdale where John kept and signed the accounts. They both moved around a bit; Abraham visited Halifax and probably Hull. John certainly visited Hull and made an annual trip to London for which in 1644 he had £3 'for expences' and an extra £1 'to spend on'. On that occasion he seems to have used Abraham's horse. These annual trips to London were to settle accounts with the partners' London factor, William Ryder. Ryder's expenses included 'hollaidge [hallage]', so presumably he was a Blackwell Hall factor.[5] Nothing seems to be known of him beyond the fact that he had a brother Joseph who lived in Lancashire.[6] There is no direct evidence that Joseph was engaged in the cloth trade, but he was certainly an intermediary through whom William Ryder transmitted money by bill to the partners. These kinship links between the provinces and London seem to have been common at all periods. Considering the constant migration to London this is not surprising, but such links would be worth fuller study.

The accounts of the partnership run from March 1644 to July 1651, but they are incomplete for the last two years. The individual accounts each cover a period of about a year, except for 1645–6 when the account runs from March 1645 to May 1646. They give a very full picture of the cloth sent to Ryder from March 1644 to August 1650, specifying the type and number of the cloths, the days on which they were dispatched and the price at which the cloth was 'sent'. In some cases the actual cost of the cloth is given, and this often differs from the price at which the cloth was sent. Thus on 7 July 1645 the following entries occur: '7 wts [whites] G.R. cost £22 sent at £22 12s' and '8 bays E.R. cost 58s apeece sent at £23 17s'. The difference between 'cost' and 'sent at' is usually 12s to 13s a pack (or 1s 6d to 1s 8d a cloth), which suggests that it represents some cost of carriage, but this is unlikely for two reasons. Firstly, in some cases there is no difference between the 'cost' and 'sent at' price, and secondly Ryder seems to have paid the cost of carriage and included it in his expenses of factorage, carriage and other charges. It is just possible that the difference between 'cost' and 'sent at' represented some cost of finishing the cloth. The difference is too small for the 'sent at' price to represent what the partners hoped to get for the cloth. In calculating the price of cloth, the 'sent at' price has been used because this is given for every consignment whereas the 'cost' is often not given.

Over the period March 1644 to August 1650 the partners sent to London 5,119 cloths, comprising 2,960 whites, 1,930 bays, 139 kerseys, forty-one and a half friezes, twenty-one greys, eleven and a half kersey friezes, one cotton, and fifteen uncertain or unspecified.[7] Thus the trade was entirely in what the accounts describe as 'peeces of woollens', for the single cotton was the woollen cloth of that name. But 'peeces of woollens' is rather misleading. The whites were certainly woollen cloth and were apparently a kind of cottons, but the bays were made with a worsted warp and a woollen weft.[8] The kerseys, friezes and greys were all woollens. Very occasionally the cloths were described as 'very good', 'speciall good ones', 'course' and 'low priced' but their general quality is better indicated by their average price in 1644–5: whites £3 1s 6d, bays £2 14s 5d, kerseys £1 13s 8d, greys £4 10s 6d and the solitary cotton £2. Later prices show that the friezes were worth £6 to £9 each[9] and the kersey friezes £5 5s 6d.

The cloth was sent to William Ryder who sold it on commission, but unfortunately his commission or factorage is nowhere given as a separate item; it cannot be disentangled from the general heading of 'factridge, cariag and all other charges of the cloth'. He certainly sold much of the cloth on credit, and in each complete account there is a list of purchasers who owed for cloth with the amounts they owed. In the list for 1644–5 there were thirty-five names, and the total amount owed was £1,726 2s. It is clear that the partners had no direct contact with their London customers, who paid for their cloth through Ryder. This helps to confirm Miss Mann's view that direct contact between clothiers and their London customers was ceasing at the time of the Civil War.[10] The accounts are not easy to understand or to disentangle, but two things are clear from them: the rise in the price of cloth and the fall in the profits from the sale of the cloth. In the period March 1644 to February 1645 the partners sent 664 cloths to Ryder, but he must have had large stocks on hand, for according to his account he had sold 1,299½ cloths,[11] which had been received at £3,533 16s 9d (or £2 14s 4d a cloth)[12] and sold at £4,466 15s (or £3 8s 8d a cloth), a difference of 26 per cent. After deducting £320 16s for factorage, carriage and other charges, the 'cleere profett' was £612 0s 3d or 17·3 per cent. Such a profit was not to be achieved again. In the succeeding and longer accounting period from March 1645 to May 1646, 1,673 cloths were sent at an average price of £3 3s 10¾d a cloth; all but one were sold, but the selling price was only £3 12s 0¼d a cloth or 12·7 per cent above the cost. After deducting £388 13s 8d for factorage, carriage and other charges, the clear profit was only £307 1s 4d or 5.6 per cent. At the same time the amount owed by the purchasers of the cloth had risen from the £1,726 2s of 1644–5 to £3,366 14s 4d. This included such sizeable sums as £465 15s 8d owed by Thomas Player, £270 8s by William Allett and £252 9s by Lancelot Toulson. There were forty-eight debtors in all.

This narrowing margin between the buying and the selling price of the cloth continued. In the period from June 1646 to June 1647 the average cost exceeded £4 a cloth; in that year 838½ cloths were sent to Ryder at a total cost of £3,365 16s 6d or £4 0s 3¾d a cloth. Of these, 755½ were sold for £3,191 17s 6d or £4 4s 6¼d a cloth, a difference of only 5.3 per cent. The eighty-three unsold cloths were then overvalued at £396 (or £4 9s 9d a cloth) and this was added to the receipts from sales to make £3,587 17s 6d. After deducting £152 19s for factorage, carriage and other charges, the net receipts were £3,434 18s 6d or £69 2s above the cost of the cloth. Thus the 'cleere proffett' was £69 2s. However the accounting is interpreted, it cannot make this into a good year for the partners. They may have found some consolation in the fact that the debts owing for cloth had fallen to £2,306 17s 10d. The following year, from July 1647 to June 1648, was not a good year either, though it was marked by a fall in the price of the cloth sent to Ryder. According to John Rodes the partners sent 639½ cloths for a total of £2,487 9s or £3 17s 10d a cloth. According to Ryder he received 687½ cloths which, with those he had on hand unsold, resulted in the sale of 790 cloths for £3,314 or £4 3s 10¾d a cloth. It is impossible to reconcile these figures, or to see how Ryder could claim that the clear profit was only £37 8s after deducting expenses of £140 18s for carriage and factorage. Indeed at this point the accounts become incoherent. In the following year (June 1648 to July 1649) when 596 cloths were sent for £2,113 9s or £3 10s 10¾d a cloth, there is no record of how many were sold or at what price. There is the rather sad comment by John Rodes that 'the 3rd. parte of proffett of cloth this yeere I supose will bee £40 for my parte', and his statement that £2,246 17s 4d was 'resting' in Ryder's hands 'all debts paid besyde the proffett of 596 peeces in 81 packes of cloth that belonges to Ab. and John Rodes'. Ryder in his terse accounts preferred to leave a blank opposite the entry 'Restinge nowe in my handes all debtes and engagements by them beinge payd'. Even so the trade continued. Between July 1649 and August 1650 704½ cloths were sent to Ryder for a total of £2,547 6s, or £3 12s 4¼d a cloth, but there is no evidence of their fate. Though details are lacking, it is clear that the trade continued until at least July 1651 when the record ends.

It is a puzzling record, at once illuminating and obscure. It is illuminating in the precision and detail with which the consignments of cloth are described; it is obscure on the profits of the trade and on the reasons for their decline. If the accounts are to be believed, the profit was £612 0s 3d in 1644–5 and then steadily declined to £37 8s in 1647–8. Even if these figures have to be taken with a grain of salt, for John Rodes was assuming a profit of £120 in 1648–9, there is really no doubt that profits declined considerably. It is true that there was some decline in the volume of trade after May 1646, but the decisive factor seems to have been a sharp rise in the cost of the cloth which was not accompanied by a corresponding rise in the selling price. The buying prices of the two main types of cloth were as follows:[13]

	whites			bays		
	£	s	d	£	s	d
March 1644–Feb. 1645	3	1	6	2	14	5
March 1645–May 1646	3	5	0	3	3	1
June 1646–May 1647	4	1	0	3	11	1
July 1647–June 1648	4	1	10	3	8	4
July 1648–June 1649	3	14	9	3	4	9
July 1649–Aug. 1650	3	15	7	3	5	4

Thus whites rose in price by 24.6 per cent between 1645–6 and 1646–7 and bays by 15.9 per cent between 1644–5 and 1645–6. There does not seem to be any very close correlation between these changing cloth prices and either the general price index or the index of wool prices. The index of 'consumables' rose sharply after 1646, but it continued to rise until 1650,[14] whereas the cloth prices fell after July 1648. From the partners' point of view the rising cost of their cloth would not have mattered so much if the selling price had risen in proportion. But it obviously did not, and again the reasons for this are not known. Of the cloth sent in 1646–7, when the cost first exceeded £4 a cloth, some remained unsold, but it seems to have been sold during the following year. If the cloth sent to London were destined for export, then the difficulties of cloth exporters at this time might produce a fall in the demand for cloth and a squeeze on the suppliers' profit margin. This would fit in with Scott's gloomy picture of economic conditions in the 1640s[15] and with the effects on foreign trade of Royalist privateering and French hostility.[16] But too little is known of the export trade at this time for any very firm conclusions to be drawn. No doubt cloth merchants experienced fluctuations in their profits, as did other merchants, and it is perhaps asking too much of seventeenth-century accounts that they should reveal the underlying reasons for such fluctuations.

The partners' accounts may not plumb the depths of economic causation, but they are illuminating on the actual mechanics of the cloth trade. They show not only what cloth was sent to Ryder but also how the return payments were made. Except on three occasions Ryder never made such payments directly in goods, for the partners' London trade was largely a one-way traffic in cloth. It was not entirely a trade in goods to London, for the partners sent to Ryder considerable sums in bills of exchange and cash. These remittances amounted to £680 in 1645–6, when they included £100 'received by William Ryder of Collonell Ashton which money I [John Rodes] repaid to Joseph Ryder', and a bill of exchange for £200 sent to Ryder 'to bee paid to him by Joseph Hunton at 3 days affter sight', which money John Rodes had 'paid here to Mr Wrigley'. The following year £424 was remitted, including £100 in cash which was sent up to London by a carrier, Lawrence Tattersall. A further £100 was sent in the same way in 1647–8 when a total of £940 was remitted, which included another bill for £200 charged on Joseph Hunton for money paid to Henry Wrigley. Finally in 1648–9 'sent Mr Ryder by bills and money and money by exchange' amounted to £530 and included £100 in cash sent on 20 February 1649 'by Sam Booth in a packe of bayes'.

When remittances of this size were added to the amounts that Ryder had to remit for the cloth he had sold, it is not surprising that he should have had to send very large sums on the partners' account. These amounted to £2,744 in 1644–5, £5,374 in 1645–6, £4,964 in 1646–7, £2,837 in 1647–8 and £2,748 in 1648–9. A very small part of these sums was paid in cash either to John Rodes on his visits to London, for example £10 in June 1646 and £163 in July 1647, or to the carriers.[17] A still smaller part was, on three occasions, remitted by Ryder in goods. The remainder was remitted by bills of exchange, a process John Rodes described as 'charghed of Mr. Ryder . . . by severall men at severall tymes', and Ryder more tersely as 'For soe much paid them by bills of exchange'. John Rodes recorded these transactions in the form '13 Aprill 1646 charghed Mr. Ryder to pay to Mr. John Vernam by the apoyntment of Mr. Ab. Hamer the some of fiffty three poundes at 10 days affter sight'. Opposite this entry is the statement that £53 had been received from Hamer in three instalments between 13 April and 19 May 1646. The largest of these transactions was on 14 July 1646 when Ryder was 'charghed' to pay £985 to Edmund Pollerd (or Pollard), who seems to have been a Warrington man. Most of these transactions were simply a way of overcoming the financial frictions of distance. Thus Ryder was regularly charged to pay money to Samuel Wyld 'or to his assignes' or to named persons 'by the apoyntment of Mr. Sam. Wyld'. Samuel Wyld was almost certainly the Rochdale mercer of that name.[18] When on 1 July 1648 Ryder was charged to pay £30 to Mr Harwell, £40 to Mr Goodfellow, £23 to Mr John Vernon and £19 to Mr Thomas Walton 'for the use of Mr. Sam Wyld', he was probably paying Wyld's debts to his London suppliers. The Rodes partners duly collected the money from Wyld 'at severall tymes'.

Apart from illustrating the financial mechanism of the inland trade, these bill transactions throw some light on the trade in goods. Thus in March 1646, when Ryder was charged to pay £150 to John Sharples, most of the money (£148 13s) was to pay for forty-four bays supplied by Sharples to the partners. A similar payment of £200 to James Ryley the following month was also for bays. Others who were paid in this way for the cloth they supplied included Robert Milnes, James Sagger (£30 in June and £60 in August 1648), Thomas Spencer (£50 in July and £10 in August 1650) and Henry Romsbotham (£50 in June 1650). The size of these payments suggests that the Rodes partners got their cloth not directly from the weavers, who would have required small regular payments, but from other clothiers. Little is known in detail about the organisation of the cloth industry in east Lancashire at this time, but large purchases of cloth from individuals do not fit in with a picture of buying and selling at the weekly cloth markets, unless those individuals were either buying up cloth from weavers or were themselves operating an extensive putting-out system on the Wiltshire model. It seems more likely that the partners bought their cloth from other clothiers who, while perhaps making some themselves, also bought up cloth from weavers. The details of the cloth sent to Ryder include its provenance. This is given in the form either of initials,[19] for example '8 bays A.W.' on 30 April 1644, or sometimes of names, as on 26 July 1644 '7 wts [whites] T. Spencer, 5 grayes George Milnes' or on 16 October 1644 '28 bayses bought of Nickolas Haworth cost dressed and redy the some of £80 10s'. Unfortunately names are rare, and it is not clear to whom the initials relate, but in 1644–5 G.R. supplied forty-nine whites and E.S. ninety-eight whites and fourteen bays, which again suggests that the partners were buying their cloth from middlemen rather than from the actual makers. Apart from the quantities, it is unlikely that E.S. would make both whites and bays.

There is no evidence that the partners made any cloth themselves,[20] but the accounts show that they bought wool in considerable quantities. On three occasions William Ryder was charged to send wool. On 30 August 1647 John Rodes 'charghed on Mr. Ryder that I bid hime buy some wooll in London to the vallewe of £50 15s 11d which hee did and sent me 4 packs'. A further three packs value £35 16s 7d followed in September. On 13 December 1647 Ryder was charged 'to buy some cotten wooll to the vallew of 3 packes'. The three packs, value £28 5s, were duly sent. This is the only reference to cotton wool in the accounts. More wool may have come from London by one of the carriers, James Breirley. On 4 April 1646 Ryder was charged to pay £24 to

James Breirley 'which hee is to bringe me wool for'. Breirley brought wool worth £230 in 1646, but it is possible that some of this was bought on the journey back to Rochdale. Widow Selby 'in Barnaby Street' and her sons Jacob and Isaac also supplied wool, to the value of £66 in 1645, £64 in 1647, £210 in 1649 and £116 in 1650. There were provincial suppliers too. The partners bought wool costing £100 from Randle Lowatt of Newcastle in 1649; in 1650 William Francke of Leicester supplied wool costing £349 and William Arnold of Coventry wool costing £50. It is not always possible to tell where the sellers of wool lived, but an important source of supply seems to have been Hull. Henry Bernard (or Barnard) of Hull supplied wool for £60 in 1646 and for £210 in 1647, but the chief Hull supplier was Captain Robert Beryor,[21] who had considerable undefined business dealings with the partners. He seems to have been authorised to take up specified sums by drawing on the partners' account with Ryder. These sums were then paid to the partners either in cash or in bills of exchange or in wool. On one occasion John Rodes collected £80, apparently in cash, from Beryor in Hull, and in July 1645 Beryor sent £50 to Halifax where Abraham Rodes collected it. Cash also seems to have been sent by carriers from Hull to Rochdale. The consignments of wool appear to have started in February 1646 when the partners received nineteen packs from Beryor consisting of seventeen packs fleece wool containing 16 stones to a pack 'bate 2 stones', at 15s stone, and two packs 'sorteinges' at £3 5s a pack, making £209 in all. Unfortunately this is the only example of a consignment being described in detail, and it would be impossible in other cases to work out prices from packs of unspecified size even when the number of packs is given, which is not often. Later consignments from Beryor were smaller, amounting to £100 in November 1646, £137 in April 1647 and £100 in May 1651. It is possible that other consignments of wool, for example from Captain Helmer in 1647–8 and from Captain Lewen in 1645 and 1648–50, were from Hull. There is no evidence on how the partners disposed of their wool, which only appears incidentally in the accounts as one of the methods of receiving payment for their cloth. At least this wool trade shows once again that the Lancashire woollen cloth industry drew its chief raw material from a wide area.

Just as the accounts throw some incidental light on the wool trade, so too they reveal something of the transport system which underlay the inland trade. The cloths were sent to London in packs, almost invariably of seven or eight whites or seven or eight bays to a pack, or eleven kerseys.[22] They were wrapped in pack cloths, some of which were, rather surprisingly, bought in London at 4s to 4s 6d a cloth. Some were bought from 'a man at Queenes Armes in Gratia Street'. Perhaps they were second-hand, for pack cloths or wrappers, which carriers were supposed to bring back, sometimes got 'lost'. The uniform size of the packs may indicate that they were sent by pack-horse rather than by wagon. They were certainly sent by a number of carriers whose names are usually given. In March, April, June and October 1644 the packs were 'sent to Hull and soe to London'. They went by carrier to Hull and 'by shipping from Hull'. By December 1644 they were being sent by land to London, and on three occasions down to February 1645 it was said that they were sent 'to Lester and soe to London'. The cost of the land carriage to Hull was 11s a pack, and the 'charges' at Hull seem to have been 11s 8d a pack. It is not clear what these charges were, but they may have been the cost of carriage by sea from Hull to London. Whatever they were, both they and the cost of land carriage to Hull down to 6 June 1644 were paid by Abraham Rodes and then recovered from Ryder by John Rodes in London and 'brought whom [home] and paid to my father because he layd it out here'. No doubt Ryder later included the amount in his general expenses for factorage, carriage and other charges.

The use of the Hull route may have been temporary and dictated by the political and military situation in 1644, for there is no clear evidence of its use after October 1644. It is not possible to be quite certain about this. After February 1645 the route is only specified in three cases, when it was by way of Leicester. On the other hand the presence of some of the carriers in London, where they had dealings with Ryder, strongly suggests that the cloth went overland all the way.[23] Moreover the timing of some of the journeys suggests this too. Thus the carrier James Breirley took cloth on 29 September, 28 October and 25 November 1645, while John Winterbotham took it on 15 September, 14 October, 12 November and 10 December 1645. This sort of shuttle service at monthly intervals would be compatible with journeys to London. It is not certain how long the round trip took. On 12 March 1646

116

James Breirley took seven packs of cloth to London where he was instructed to buy wool; he delivered the wool on 4 April. In the summer of the same year he made the round trip between 14 July and 3 August. In the autumn a slightly better time was recorded. Breirley left with six packs on 1 October 1646 and was in London on 10 October when he received £28 from Ryder to buy wool; the partners received the wool from him on 20 October. It must be admitted that the evidence is not always as straightforward as this. There are cases where the timing of the journeys is not consistent with a round trip to London. Thus four packs were 'sent to Breirley' on 30 March 1645 and a further six packs on 6 April; he could not have got to London and back in eight days. But did he actually leave on 30 March or did he wait for a week to pick up the other six packs? These cases are rare, and not enough is known about the carrying business to be sure what they mean. For example, did a carrier always accompany the packs entrusted to him, or did he sometimes send them by one of his men? One of the carriers, Raphe Lees, was taking cloth in 1649–50, and on 9 July 1650 four packs were sent by 'Raphe Lees man'. On three occasions in all John Rodes recorded the carriage of cloth by 'my man George Knowles' and 'my man Edward', but this was very exceptional, for the partners were almost wholly dependent on the professional carriers. These carriers did not leave on a fixed day of the week,[24] though if the dates are to be believed, Breirly usually left on a Saturday, Monday or Tuesday. Allowing for a brief stop in London and allowing time for the 'turn round' at Rochdale, the dates on which cloth was sent suggest that the journey to London or the journey back could be done in seven to ten days. Unfortunately it is impossible to discover what this carriage cost.

The finer details of the carriers' business may not be very clear, but it appears that their work was not really seasonal. They carried the cloth all the year round, as the accompanying table [p. 118] shows.

The table presents some interesting and puzzling features. It does not suggest that carriage was much influenced by climatic conditions. It could be argued that the low figures for November and December reflected the English winter, but the English winter is usually worse after the New Year than before it, and the figures for January to March are above the monthly average. It is just possible that the monthly figures are a reflection of the

	1645	1646	1647	1648	1649	Totals
January	7	14	14	10	4	49
February	8	20	7	6	3	44
March	6	20	18	4	15	63
April	15	17	7	10	2	51
May	27	18	7	9	6	67
June	14	7	0	8	15	44
July	18	6	6	11	0	41
August	8	18	4	13	9	52
September	17	0	8	4	2	31
October	16	13	21	8	2	60
November	11	14	0	0	3	28
December	5	6	0	0	8	19

methods of cloth production. If the cloth were made by people who combined farming with their cloth making, it might be argued that the cloth output would vary in inverse ratio to agricultural activity. Thus more cloth would be made in the winter months and would come onto the market in the spring, which could account for the high figures of March to May. A fall in production in the busier agricultural months might then account for the low figures of June to September, which are below the average at a time when transport conditions should have been good. Only the high figure for October does not fit into this pattern. Perhaps the pattern itself is fanciful, but there can be a rhythm in domestic industry, as the hand-knitted stocking industry shows, and there the rhythm arose from the combination of agricultural and industrial work.[25] It is at least possible that similar conditions were found in the east Lancashire cloth industry at a time when both agriculture and industry were very labour-intensive.

The records of the Rodes partnership illustrate those links between the Rochdale cloth industry and its London market to which Wadsworth drew attention more than forty years ago. They show that the trade continued during the last years of the first Civil War. Even the shipments through Hull may not have been a purely wartime measure, and certainly the trading links with Hull, for example in wool, continued after 1645. Moreover the partners made their highest profits during the closing years of the first Civil War. The subsequent rise in the cost of cloth and decline in profits may have resulted from a combination of internal conditions of production and external conditions of demand. But not enough is known about either for firm conclusions to be drawn. In Professor Fisher's 'Dark Ages in English economic history', the years from 1640 to 1660 are some of the darkest.

Notes

1 For a survey of some aspects of the economy see J. P. Cooper, 'Social and economic policies under the Commonwealth' in G. E. Aylmer, ed., *The Interregnum: The quest for settlement 1646–1600*, pp. 121–42.

2 The accounts are in the Manchester City Library, Archives Dept., MS. M 1/26. They were originally part of the City archives, but there is no evidence on how they came to be there.

3 On the Rochdale cloth industry see A. P. Wadsworth and J. de L. Mann, *The cotton trade and industrial Lancashire 1600–1780*, book I; A. P. Wadsworth, 'The history of the Rochdale woollen trade', *Trans. Rochdale Literary and Scientific Soc.*, xv (1925), 90–110, and 'Sidelights on Rochdale history', *ibid.*, xvi (1928), 55–73.

4 Rodes in its various forms (Roades, Roads etc) is a fairly common Lancashire name, and it is difficult to disentangle the Rochdale Rodeses; Abraham may have been born in 1585, Samuel in 1615, John in 1619 and Abel in 1622 (H. Fishwick, *The registers of the parish church of Rochdale, 1582 to 1616*, pp. 12, 158, *1617 to 1641*, pp. 19, 32).

5 For the activities of the Blackwell Hall factors in the seventeenth century see J. de L. Mann, *The cloth industry in the West of England from 1640 to 1880*, pp. 63–77.

6 William may have been the William Rider of St Giles, Cripplegate, London, citizen and clothworker, whose will was proved 1 March 1666 (P.C.C. Mico f. 50).

7 Consisting of eight whites and bays and seven 'severall sorts'.

8 Dr Bowden seems to accept too readily the clothiers' claim that bays were 'only cottons' and contained no worsted yarn (P. J. Bowden, *The wool trade in Tudor and Stuart England*, p. 56).

For a discussion of this see Wadsworth and Mann, *op. cit.*, pp. 13–14.

[9] These prices show that all Lancashire cloth was not coarse and cheap as is sometimes supposed. The kersey, a light cloth, was the really cheap cloth; it never exceeded £2 4s a cloth in the Rodes accounts.

[10] J. de L. Mann, *op. cit.*, p. 65.

[11] Actually thirty-one cloths remained unsold, but their value (£100) was included in the calculation of profit.

[12] This implies that the cloth on hand had cost less than the cloth sent in 1644–5, for the latter cost £2 18s 6d a cloth.

[13] These are the prices at which the cloth was 'sent' (fractions of a penny omitted). The monthly variations in price do not show any seasonal trend.

[14] E. H. Phelps Brown and S. V. Hopkins, 'Seven centuries of the prices of consumables, compared with builders' wage-rates' in E. M. Carus-Wilson, ed., *Essays in economic history*, ii. 195.

[15] W. R. Scott, *The constitution and finance of English, Scottish, and Irish joint-stock companies to 1720*, i. 230–43.

[16] J. P. Cooper, *op. cit.*, p. 123.

[17] It is not always possible to be sure whether the carriers were carrying cash or bills. Very occasionally they brought back small amounts of tobacco, as 2 lb at 8s lb in May 1647.

[18] J. P. Earwaker, ed., *Lancashire and Cheshire wills and inventories, 1572–1696*, Chetham Society, n.s., 28 (1893), pp. 207–8.

[19] Occasionally the initials look more like cloth or merchants' marks.

[20] There is a single reference to them paying £10 for dyeing.

[21] Presumably the Robert Berrier who was surety for £200 owed to Trinity House, Hull, in 1651 (F. W. Brooks, ed., *The first Order Book of Hull Trinity House 1632–1665*, Yorks. Arch. Soc. Record Series, cv (1942), 105.

[22] A pack of eleven kerseys would weigh about 220 lb. Friezes were sent at five to six to a pack which would weigh 220–264 lb, if the cloth were of the statutory weight.

[23] Thomas Priestley of Soyland near Halifax took cloth to London by land 'with 8 or 9 horses all the time of the Civil War' (C. Jackson, ed., *Yorkshire diaries and autobiographies*, ii, Surtees Soc., lxxvii (1883), 23).

[24] They very rarely left on a Sunday, though 30 March and 6 April

1645 were Sundays.

25 T. S. Willan, *An eighteenth-century shopkeeper: Abraham Dent of Kirkby Stephen*, pp. 64, 110. Dr Thirsk has suggested that when goods were produced for export and such export 'continued all the year round', then the production of such goods would not be seasonal (J. Thirsk, 'The fantastical folly of fashion' in N. B. Harte and K. G. Ponting, eds., *Textile history and economic history*, p. 64). But seasonal production is not incompatible with export all the year round any more than the seasonal wool clip is incompatible with the continuous production of cloth.

V TWO LONDON WHOLESALERS

The northern clothiers sent their cloth to London as a centre of consumption and of export, but the capital was also a centre for the distribution of goods to other parts of the country. The most obvious example of this is the distribution of imported wares, such as groceries and wine, which were re-shipped coastwise from London. Less obvious is the role of London in the purely internal trade of the country. Clearly some cloth was sent to London and consumed there, but was some also sent for further distribution in the counties around the capital? This might be more likely to occur where such further distribution could be effected by water rather than by land carriage. This is what happened in the case of goods destined for export, but the channelling of so much foreign trade through London could hardly be matched by a similar concentration of internal trade. The cost of transport, especially of land carriage, might favour a direct route between producer and consumer, rather than an indirect link through an entrepot. Even so, there were centres of regional distribution such as Bristol in the west, and presumably London played a similar role in the east, even if little is known in detail about it. Indeed rather more is known about London as a centre for the distribution of imported goods than about London as a centre for the distribution of native commodities, whether produced in the capital itself or brought there from the provinces. In either case very little work has been done on the actual methods by which goods were distributed from London to the provinces. Was the London wholesaler a 'sedentary' merchant either expecting his provincial customers to come to him or employing agents in the provinces who would keep in touch with such customers; or was he an 'itinerant' merchant who went himself with his goods into the provinces? It would seem that all these methods were employed, but the itinerant wholesaler probably confined his travelling to attending fairs in person with his goods. One such itinerant London merchant or shopkeeper has left some record of his attendance at fairs in letters written home to his wife.

These letters, with one exception, were written by Robert Gray to his 'lovinge wyffe' Anne between 1606 and 1618.[1] Gray had a shop in London, but his letters say very little about the nature of his trade. He certainly bought cloth, including undyed says which he had dyed, durance from Norwich and kerseys. It does not seem that he bought this cloth at the fairs he attended, nor is there any evidence of what he actually sold at the fairs. On 6 December 1606 Gray wrote to his wife from Exeter, where he was attending the St Nicholas Fair, and sent her 'for a token' some lace, which he had bought from 'my Ante Symonds', and 10s in gold out of which and out of her own bounty she was to 'bestow upon my mother a pynt of Cannary and drenke to us'. He also sent her a bill of exchange for £10, presumably an inland bill, with instructions 'I pray let Trustrom[2] receve yt and for the other monyes I hope he hath receved, and payd such monyes as I welled hem to paye; I praye yf he have receved any store of monyes more than I left hem order to paye, that you would kepe it in your kepinge and see that he doth receve yt just and good monyes'. Gray was anxious about the shop and entreated his wife 'to be as much in the shope as well you maye and put the folks in mynde of ther besynes other wayes yt will not be well performed by them as yt should be, for they ar verye neclygent in ther besynes and doth yt by halffes'. By 14 February 1607 Gray was back in Exeter, presumably for the Ash Wednesday Fair; his father had also just arrived there, though they had not travelled down together. Again Gray sent his wife a token, a small piece of gold, 'as from the trewe love of my hart to you'. Again he was worried about the shop and entreated his wife 'to be as much in the shope as you well maye and see that when any of the folks doth goe forth of dores you know whether they goe and that they make noe longer staye then nedes they must, and when they receve any mony praye your mother to take yt, that yt doe not lye about the shope, wherby ther should be any wantes'. She was also to 'see that the folks have a care that the shope and wyndowes be made fast at nyght, and that they gett such things redy as is nedfull'. Gray 'would not have Wench[3] forth of dores yf any chapmen should com the while, for Trustrom doth not knowe them; I pray see that when any of our costomares com to London that Wench be verye carfull to sarve them that ar good men; and for the other lett them goe'. Finally Anne was to 'lett not my lettares be cast about but sett up saffe'.

In 1608 Gray attended two of the Exeter fairs, in May and August. On the latter occasion he had come on from Bristol, presumably after attending the St James's Fair there. On 2 August 1608 he wrote to his wife from Exeter saying that he made 'accownt to ryde further west' before returning, and that he found 'monyes verye hard to com bey'. A year later he was on the Bristol-Exeter circuit again, this time accompanied by his brother, and was again sending his wife tokens 'in gould', one of which was taken to London by his father. On this occasion he must have been away from home for at least three weeks. In July 1610 Gray was in Bristol and from there he sent his wife 'five bills of exchange' which George was 'to receve in the monyes for'. He also sent 'per Mr Brach the bedell of the Gerdlares Hall ij lettares of advice to receve the monyes'. George was 'to be carfull of his besnyes', and as the money came in he was to 'sett yt up and see how yt doth goe forth and to whom'. George was also 'to sell Umphrey Sydnam noe wares except he doth com of hem selffe'. Sydnam had returned from Bristol to London apparently leaving his business in Gray's hands, who had 'sould hem a gredell [great deal?] of wares' at Bristol. Down in Bristol Gray had still to bear in mind his London stock. He gave instructions that John Ven should buy '30 or 35 peces of sayes' and dye them 'the collours I wrought of' and should 'speke to Danyell Mr Facetts man of Norwich for 30 or 40 peces of durence'. There is no evidence of Gray's attendance at fairs in 1611, but on 25 May 1612 'thanks be geven to God' he 'came saffe and well to Exeter', where his brother had already arrived.

The timing of fairs sometimes made it difficult for Gray to fit them into his itinerary. In May 1613 he was at Beverley, no doubt for the great Cross Fair there, and wrote to his wife on the 12th praying her to ask his brother to go to Exeter, for 'Trustrom wrights me that my brother must neds be at Exeter, and in respacke that he doth goe I will not be ther this fayer my selffe, I make no dowte but my brother will carfulley respacke my besynes in my absence for yt is not without ned for sarvants ar necleygent, and the cheffest of the fayre wilby there at the verye ferst'. It would have been difficult for Gray to have got from Beverley to Exeter for the 'cheffest' of the Whit Monday Fair. By 24 July 1613 Gray was in Bristol where he 'and all myne with our goods' had come safe and well, as had his father. The journey down had not been uneventful for 'the watares ware so hey that wee had much adoe to pase in many places for water, and corne very dere, but thanks be to God this 6 dayes of fayer wether hath made corn to fall ijs. in a bosell here and is lycke to fall more every daye'. As so often Gray reminded his wife of her 'carfulness to the shope in my absence'. He hoped that the fair, which was 'newly begone' would 'prove resonabell good', but moneys were 'very carse [scarce?]'. Finally Anne's maid Margery was to have a care to his clothes that they 'be kept in good order', and if Mr Edmonds was not yet 'in hand with your garden', Anne was to 'lett yt rest untell my cominge hom because I would see yt effecktyalley done my selffe'. Gray had missed the Whitsuntide Fair at Exeter but he was back there in December 1613 for the St Nicholas Fair which, he reported laconically', 'doth fall out as in formor tymes'. By 4 December he had finished his business at the fair and was going to make all haste home. His wife was to 'tell the folks that I wright you I shalbe at hom on Satterday because they wilbe the more myndfull of there besynes, but yt wilbe the Thursday after this doth com to your hands and then God wellen I hope to be with you'.

There are no letters from Gray in 1614–15, but he wrote to his wife from Bristol on 23 July 1616 explaining that he would have written before but he had 'ben very much trobelled with sore eyes'. He was troubled too about his sister, whom he had visited at Windsor on the way down and who lived 'very much dyscontented with her mistress'. His father intended 'to have her home as he doth com hom wards'. Gray was also worried by a letter he had received from 'my man Georg' telling him 'Mrs Walker of Hull appoynted me xxiij li, so because he could not com to her bill he could not have the mony'. 'I showed you', Gray informed his wife, 'the mornynge beffore I cam awaye wher you should have all the bills, this is som hendrance that the bill was not locked for, so God knowes howe longe I shalbe without my mony, you shall here more at large per the next from me'. In the meantime Anne was prayed to 'have a care to the shope for you knowe howe sympell they be which ar at hom with you'. Despite his obvious displeasure, Gray remained 'your ever lovinge husband duryng lyffe'. This was the last letter from Gray to his wife that has survived, but on 24 September 1618 Gray wrote from London 'to his sarvant Ames Baker' at Chester. He reported that he had 'spoken with Mr. Richard Baker but noe mony here is to be had ... you know I gott lettell by the wares he had of me at St Poles fayer and also by the £200 of wares he had at St James tyde before, which is in all nere £400, and as that I have receved but £50 of Mr. Tho. Hart'. There are no details of these wares, but they show something of the scale on which Gray operated. This final letter shows that Gray was embarking on a new venture; he was sending Ames over to Dublin to trade on his behalf, and was full of apprehension over 'this jorny I send you' where 'the danger and the charge is great every waye both out and home'. He had sent Ames a pack of wares weighing 2 cwt, on which the carriage was 13s 4d; they were 'a parsell of extreordynary good wares'. With a final injunction 'to effecke all besynes throughley', the letter and the record end.

These letters are of interest quite apart from their rarity value. They show the importance of the fair in the distribution of goods from London into the provinces, even if their lack of detail reveals little of the nature of Gray's trade. It is probable that he sold goods both retail and wholesale at his London shop, though the references to chapmen and to customers coming to London suggest a wholesale trade. He may have sold by retail at the fairs he attended, but the references to bills of exchange and the rare examples of the scale of his transactions again strongly suggest that he was selling wholesale. Whatever the exact nature of his trade, Gray's attendance at the Bristol, Exeter and Beverley Fairs shows one way by which a London retailer or wholesaler could penetrate the provincial market. There were other ways of doing this as the activities of a London merchant, Giles Pooley, show. Pooley's accounts for the years 1654–8 have in part survived, and they provide a much fuller picture of a London wholesaler at work than can be drawn from Gray's letters.[4]

Nothing seems to be known about Giles Pooley apart from what can be learned from his accounts which include personal as well as business items. He was apparently a widower who 'broke up howse keeping' in April 1653 when he went to lodge with a business associate, Robert Carter. He paid Carter £20 per annum for 'dyet, loging & c.', and £8 per annum for 'provition of clothes', which sounds an odd arrangement. These payments did not include laundry, for Goodwife or Goody Spring was paid regularly for washing Pooley's clothes; she charged about 3s a month for this, and was paid roughly every quarter. She may also have received the odd 4d for mending his stockings. Pooley seems to have been heavy on shoes, for 'John Peerce shooemaker' was paid £1 18s 6d on 1 April and £1 3s on 24 October 1654. Pooley had a daughter who appears in the accounts simply as E. Pooley. She, too, was boarded out, with a Mrs Tylsed at £16 per annum. In April 1655 £2 16s was paid to M. de la Clay for tailor's work for her, and in July 1655 £8 12s was paid for silk and 14s 6d 'for a petticote' for her. Such payments do not suggest that she was a child. Pooley's dispersed rather than extended family seems to have included an apprentice, Edward Lewse, who boarded with Mr Coe, and was provided with 'a payre of bootes' in March 1655 and with sums of money when he travelled in the country on his master's business. Finally Pooley had his horses, which were also boarded out. The mare, whose 'sadle, bridle and all furniture' cost £1 16s and shoeing 2s, had her 'standing at the Swan in Coleman Street' at a cost of 10s 6d a month. That was in the summer of 1655; in November she was 'at grass one weeke' at a cost of 2s 6d and was then wintered for fifteen weeks at 1s 3d a week. In 1656 the mare's standing was transferred to the Bell in Finsbury where it cost 14s 6d a month. The 'browne nagg', which was at grass at Mile End in the summer of 1656, seems to have cost about 10s 6d a month to keep. Such charges suggest that it was not cheap to keep horses in London.

The economic basis of this two-horse standard of living was trade. Before 1654 Pooley was in partnership with William Holcroft with whom he had what was called 'a parteable accompt' which was different from the accounts that have survived. The surviving accounts are headed 'Journall for the proper accompt of Giles Pooley of London Merchant beegining in January 1653/4'. The first entry is for cloth valued at £124 11s 5d, and is headed 'Wares are Dr. to stock of Giles Pooley and are thes followeing peeces brought into stock by him uppon this new accompt, they beeing the remainder of a parcell of wares which he had uppon his owne accompt whyle he was in Company with Mr. Holcroft'. While this might imply that the partnership had been dissolved, there is some evidence that it continued and that Pooley and Holcroft had some trade together, maintaining for that purpose their partible account. Thus some cloth sent, rather surprisingly, to the Canaries in 1656 was said to stand to the credit of Pooley 'in the parteable accompt of Giles Pooley and Wm. Holcroft'.[5] Similarly a little cloth sent to 'Pharo'[6] and Virginia a year later seems to have been a joint venture on the partible account. If this partnership continued in an active form, it has not left much trace in the surviving 'proper accompt', which covers the trade Pooley conducted either on his own or with another partner. That trade included a sale of indigo at Ipswich in 1655[7] and the purchase of ninety-eight bundles of viol strings from Captain Richard Payne. They were bought at 2s 6d a bundle and sold at the same price to Captain Salmon who bought ninety bundles and to Robert Carter who bought the remaining eight. This was presumably a transaction among friends rather than a business deal, for Pooley lodged with Carter and had personal dealings with Salmon. Pooley did not make his living out of indigo and viol strings; his real trade was in cloth and wine.

As a cloth merchant Giles Pooley did not deal in the woollen cloths which formed the stock in trade of northern clothiers, but in the new draperies of eastern England. These worsted or mixed fabrics were lighter and cheaper than the traditional broadcloth. They were made extensively in Norfolk and were indeed often described as Norwich stuffs.[8] In 1654 Pooley bought most of his cloth in Norwich, where he seems to have employed an agent, Francis Dacket.[9] He received sixty-two pieces of white and mixed damask from Dacket at prices ranging from 28s to 38s a piece. The account includes 'provision at 8d per piece' which may have represented Dacket's commission. Payment for the cloth was made by bills of exchange which Dacket apparently drew on Pooley. Other cloth was supplied 'by order of F. Dacket' and in these cases the actual suppliers were named. They were Thomas Endicke and Barnard Church, both described as weavers of Norwich. Endicke supplied twenty-six pieces of mixed damask at 36s a piece and four pieces of 'whyte rashes' at 58s 6d a piece. Church supplied more expensive cloth: fine white grograms at £5 each, 'black haire russells' at £5 3s, and 'white haire russells' at £4 15s each.[10] His total bill for 1654 was £67 15s. Some of the Norwich cloth was sent to London by water at a cost of 7s cwt. This was cheap transport, for a consignment weighing 4¼ cwt and costing £104 19s 5d paid only £1 9s 9d in carriage. As the consignment consisted of sixty-two pieces of damask, each piece can only have weighed about $7\frac{1}{2}$ lb. It is not clear how much of the cloth was sent by water, but a later reference to cloth being received 'per Burry carrier' shows that some went by land. Some of Pooley's cloth was bought nearer at hand, for in 1654 he purchased a little in London itself. Most of this came from Josiah Rycraft of London, merchant, who supplied mohairs, serge, 'castillianoe',[11] 'silkes adarettos'[12] and 'French stuffe' to a total of £27 6s. Pooley was 'to pay ready money', which he did.

After 1654 the pattern of Pooley's cloth purchases changed. He now bought practically no cloth in Norwich. Indeed only a single purchase of three pieces of 'black haire itallyanoes'[13] and a piece of 'haire and silke stuffe gray'[14] from Barnard Church in 1655 can definitely be attributed to Norwich. Instead Pooley concentrated on buying from London merchants. Some of these purchases were small. Thus Henry Ballowe & Co. supplied a single piece of black worsted callimento[15] at £5 8s, Joseph Skottowe, merchant, seven pieces of black russells at £3 a piece, Oliver Phillips, merchant, six pieces of broad 'chenyes'[16] at 53s a piece and William Dey, merchant, eight pieces of the same cloth at 50s to 53s a piece. All these were bought for ready money. There were only two big London suppliers, assuming Samuel Everard was a London merchant even though he was not described as such. Everard supplied twenty pieces of 'meduces'[17] at 54s a piece on 1 September 1657 for ready money (he was paid on 19 September) and ten pieces 'picotillas or silke druggetts' at 50s each and three pieces 'silke chequarettes'[18] at 60s each for which he was to pay in three months. Finally Philip Peddar of London, merchant, was the biggest supplier of all. In January and February 1655 he sold Pooley a wide variety of cloth which included castillianoes at 38s, worsted adarettos at 38s and silk adarettos at 44s, 'mixt tammetts'[19] at 52s, white tammetts at 52s to 73s each, a 'cornation[20] in grain' tammett at 82s, black russells at 58s and ten 'mixt prunellas[21] or princes searges' at 57s. The total came to £214 2s, of which £100 was to be paid in money and 'the rest in truck for wines'. Between March and May 1655 Peddar supplied more castillianoes as well as mohairs (at 43s 6d), 'wooll druggetts' (at 70s), 'whyte broad chenyes' (at 48s) and '1 cornation in grain broad watterd cheny' (at 65s). The total was £107 7s, and all was 'in truck for wines'. Finally in 1656 Peddar supplied Pooley with twenty-two black russells at 58s, seventeen druggets at 53s, two 'mixt tammetts' at 52s and a castillianoe at 40s. There is no record of how the total of £115 11s was to be paid.

There is no evidence that Pooley bought his cloth for export, apart from his small ventures with William Holcroft to the Canaries, 'Pharo' and Virginia. He sold most of his cloth in London; the remainder was sold in the provinces. The London buyers seem to have ranged from shopkeepers to wholesalers and merchants who may have been buying for export. Thus John Chapman of London, 'sales man', bought one piece of broad mixed grogram for 64s ready money in May 1655 and one piece of mixed tammett for 53s a year later, when he was given three months to pay. Roger Hunt, also described as a 'sales man', bought six druggets at 53s, a piece of scarlet tammett at 56s and a piece of 'Turky tammett' for 38s (19 yds at 2s yd). He was to pay the total of £20 12s in three months. Only two of the buyers were described as mercers; one bought a single broad worsted grogram for £3 5s (to pay at a month) and the other, John Lane, bought castillianoes, mohairs and tammetts (mixed at 48s, coloured at 58s, flame coloured at 108s and 'aurora in grain' at 105s). He was to pay ready money for the total of £50 15s. The bigger buyers were usually described as merchants. They included Samuel Toft who bought castillianoes and mohairs for £61 4s, Henry Borneford who bought thirty pieces of 'sattinistoes'[22] at 61s, 10 'mixt druggetts' at 57s and ten 'broad chenyes' at 53s, Thomas Hopkins who bought twenty pieces of meduces at 54s a piece and Richard Baker who bought five 'broad waterd chenys' at 51s, five 'dyed barragons'[23] at 58s, ten picotillas at 57s and five 'chequarretts' at 67s. Baker's purchase was described as 'Mr Baker's parcell Norwich stuffs'. He and the other merchants were to pay ready money. Most of the cloth sold in London was for ready money, but some transactions involved an element of barter. Thus James Vaughan of London, merchant, bought cloth for £9 13s on 2 June 1654 for which he was to pay ready money. Three weeks later he made a larger purchase which came to £43 16s. This he was 'to pay ½ money in 2 months the rest per sucketts'. As a result suckets were 'Dr to James Vaughan . . . of him taken in truck for wares, and sent per J. Vaughan to Wm. Hand in Scotland, Commissary of the Army ther, with an order since to him to give accompt therof to Giles Pooley beeing for his proper accompt, they amounting to £25 1s'. William Hand as 'Dr to suckets' was to 'give an accompt' for 'the above mentioned parcell', but it is not clear that he did. Similarly Alexander Sandeland bought eighty-five pieces of damask at 34s to 41s 6d a piece, which came to £162 1s 6d in all. He was 'to pay halfe money the rest per wine'. He seems to have paid £76 in wine, comprising four butts of sherry at £19 a butt.

Pooley's sales of cloth in the provinces were small compared with his sales in London. Indeed only four provincial buyers can be identified with certainty, and three of them made only small purchases. Thus Edward Hobson of Chichester bought two pieces of 'black haire ittallyanoes' at £5 each and a mixed tammett at £3 in 1654; William Knight of Reading, who bought wine from Pooley, purchased a piece of worsted grogram for 72s in 1655; George Capell of Bristol, merchant, was sent a selection of cloth early in 1655 from which he bought only a yellow tammett and two mohairs for £7 15s and returned the rest. Perhaps Pooley had hoped that Capell would be a better customer, for the cloth sent to him apparently cost £2 15s in carriage. Finally Richard Young of Bristol was the only provincial buyer on any scale.[24] In April 1655 he bought a mixed collection of cloth—tammetts, castillianoes, it-tallyanoes and 'princes searges'—for £82 12s, for which he was to pay £50 ready money and the rest in one month.[25] In May he bought seven tammetts for £17 3s, payable in a month, and two 'wooll druggetts' at 77s and 'one cornation in grain broad watter'd cheny' for 69s, for which he was to pay ready money. All this cloth seems to have been part of that purchased by Pooley from Philip Peddar. In this case it looks very much as if Norwich stuffs reached Bristol by way of London.[26]

All this cloth trade seems to have been conducted by Giles Pooley on his own, except for his small export ventures with William Holcroft and except for a very limited partnership with Robert Carter in 1657. The latter covered only two half pieces of broadcloth bought from Major Warren for £16 8s 6d[27] and sold to Gerard Hacten for £20, two dozen pairs of worsted stockings bought for £7 10s from John Hall and sold for £8 2s to Henry Mullum, four pieces of Taunton serges bought from John Lewes for £12 and sold for £13 4s, again to Henry Mullum, and a parcel of Norwich stuffs bought for £66 11s and sold to Richard Baker for £72 10s. The total profit was £11 6s 6d, or just over 10 per cent, which was divided equally between Pooley and Carter. Unfor-tunately it is not possible to calculate with any precision what profit or loss Pooley made in the cloth trade which he conducted on his own. The accounts make no attempt whatsoever to do this; they are, as their title says, a 'Journall' or chronological list of transactions. There are fractions in the margins which seem to relate to a ledger that has not survived, and there are references to a 'petty charge booke' and a 'cash booke'. The accounts do, however, show the volume of Pooley's trade. If transactions done in partnership with Holcroft and Carter are omitted, the accounts show that Pooley bought cloth for £274 3s 6d in 1654, for £364 10s 6d in 1655, for £166 17s in 1656 and for £56 5s in 1657; he sold cloth for £305 0s 6d in 1654, for £337 13s 6d in 1655, for £181 2s in 1656 and for £63 17s in 1657. Thus he bought cloth for £862 16s and sold cloth for £887 12s in the four years. As there is no evidence that Pooley held a stock of unsold cloth in March 1658 when the accounts end, the figures would suggest a declining trade that had never been very profitable. Moreover the figures take no account of expenses which may have included some 'processing' of the cloth. Thus in March 1654 fifty-four pieces of damask were 'callendred and scrapt' at 10d a piece, and in 1657 John Brighterig, callender, was paid £1. Similarly Thomas Hall, a presser, was paid £1 4s in 1656. Finally in June 1655 £6 10s was paid to Abraham Hebert 'for worke done by him as in the workemen's booke appears'. Hebert was a dyer, and the money was paid for dyeing five pieces of tammetts, which shows how expensive dyeing could be. Such payments have obviously to be considered before counting the difference between the buying and selling price as profit.

Another approach to this problem of profit is to try to determine the difference between the buying and selling price in individual cases. This is a difficult task in the case of cloth, which could vary in quality and size; it is necessary to be sure that the cloth bought was the same as the cloth sold. It is possible to make this comparison in some of Pooley's transactions. Thus in 1654 three black hair russells were bought for £15 6s and sold for £16 12s, a difference of 8.5 per cent; three white hair russells bought for £14 5s and sold for £16 16s showed a 'profit' of 18 per cent; two cornation in grain cheyneys cost £5 16s and were sold for £6 8s, an increase of 10 per cent. But such margins seem to have been exceptional. In 1655 castillianoes were bought at 38s and sold at 38s or 39s; mohairs bought at 43s 6d sold at 44s; mixed tammetts bought at 52*s* sold at 48*s* to 50*s*; five prunellas bought at 52*s* were sold at 54*s*. In 1656 broad cheyneys were bought and sold at 53*s*, mixed tammetts were bought at 52*s* and sold at 52*s* and 53*s*. Finally in 1657 twenty meduces were bought for a total of £54 and sold for £56. It would be unwise to draw very firm conclusions from such figures, but they do seem to suggest two things. Firstly they show that the margin between the buying and the selling price varied greatly, and secondly that after 1654 the margin contracted to a point where the trade could hardly be profitable at all. The exception to this was the profit of 10 per cent which was made by the partnership of Pooley and Carter in 1657, but neither partner was passing rich on his profit of £5 13*s* 3*d*. Unless the accounts are misleading, which is always possible, they show that Pooley's own trade in cloth can have yielded little profit, and this seems confirmed by a comparison of buying and selling prices in individual transactions, at least after 1654. The reason for this remains obscure. It may have resulted not from a rise in the cost of the cloth but from a fall in the selling price, as with the Rodes partnership. This would be difficult to prove, for Pooley dealt in a large and changing variety of cloths. Of the two dozen types of cloth he bought and sold, some were bought only on one occasion and some were bought and sold only in a particular year. From such transactions it is impossible to determine any trend in either buying or selling prices; nor is it possible to do this with any conviction in other cases. The changing variety of cloths may itself have some significance. Damask, grogram and russells predominated in 1654, tammetts and castillianoes in 1655, russells and druggets in 1656 and meduces in 1657. Was Pooley trying to find the most profitable line? If he was, there is no evidence that he succeeded.

There were obvious links between this cloth trade and Pooley's trade in wine; cloth was bought from Philip Peddar partly 'in truck for wines', and cloth was sold to Alexander Sandeland partly for payment in wine. But Pooley's wine trade was greater and more complex than his cloth trade. He bought French and Spanish and Rhenish wines. The Spanish were usually described as Canary or Malaga. There is no evidence at all that Pooley imported any of his wine. He bought it from other merchants who may have been the original importers. A little wine was bought from provincial merchants. Thus Jonathan Bass of Woodbridge

supplied four butts of Malaga at £25 a butt in September 1655; he
was to be paid 'at 4 months and 4 months'.[28] Early in 1656 John
More of Ipswich supplied Canary, 'being some what more than a
hogshead' for £16. George Gosnell, also of Ipswich, supplied '4
peeces Spanish wine viz 3 pipes Mallaga and 1 butt at £24 per
peece' in October 1656. He was to be paid the £96 in two instalments, £60 in February and £36 in May 1657. He was duly
paid on time. Ipswich was the headquarters of Pooley's provincial
wine trade, and it is therefore not surprising that he should have
bought a little wine there, but his main purchases were made in
London.

The London suppliers seem to have specialised in French or
Spanish or Rhenish wine; they rarely supplied more than one
type. Less than a fifth of the wine that Pooley bought was French.
He got most of this from two London wine firms. Arnold Beake &
Co. supplied 10 tons of French wine at £11 ton[29] (payable in three
months) in May 1655; in April 1656 they supplied 3 hogsheads at
£9 a hogshead for ready money and in November of the same year
2 tons at £25 ton, payable in three months. The other firm was
Thomas Canham & Co., one of the very few supplying both
French and Spanish wines. Pooley bought from them 2 tons of
French wine at £22 a ton (payable in three months) in 1655, and 7
butts of Malaga at £22 10s butt in 1656, again payable in three
months. The relatively small purchases of French wine may
reflect not English taste but the fact that the import of French
wines was, in theory at least, prohibited between 1649 and 1657.[30]

Spanish wine was much more important, which suggests that
Cromwell's war with Spain did not at first cut off imports from
that country. Pooley bought most of his Spanish wine from about
a dozen London merchants, including Alexander Sandeland who
supplied it in truck for cloth. Thus in 1655 William Whyttle of
London, merchant, supplied 6 pipes of Canary for £138, one third
to be paid in ready money and the rest at three months and three
months; Robert Dix, wine cooper, supplied 5 butts Malaga for
£94, half payable in a month and the other half in three months;
Mathew Cape sold 4 pipes of Canary at £12 a pipe and was to be
paid 'present money'; Robert Hall, another wine cooper, supplied
a pipe of Canary for £25 ready money and a further 3 pipes of
Canary at £26 a pipe in 1656 (half ready money, half at three
months). Other suppliers in 1655 included Philip Manning whose

10 pipes of Canary cost only £13 10s a pipe, payable half at three months and half at five months (an unusual period of credit); Samuel Watson, who supplied 8 butts of Malaga at £19 a butt, payable one third ready money and the rest 'at three and three monthes', and Francis Shutlewood, whose wine was classified as Spanish and described as 'sweete' and cost about 5s 6d a gallon payable at three months. In October 1655 Edward Turbutt, wine cooper, sold '9 butts Mallaga wines excize free at £15 per butt' and was to be paid 'halfe in money and per French wine the rest at Christmas'; in fact he seems to have been paid £25 10s in French wine (1½ tons at £17 ton) and the rest in cash. After 1655 Pooley bought less Spanish wine, and only two or three big suppliers appear in the next two years. In 1656 Richard King of London, merchant, supplied '5 butts of Mallaga wines at £21 per butt wee pay excize'; this was for 'present money'. In 1657 Pooley bought '4 pipes ½ and 12 gallons of Canary at £11 per pipe' from William Sherington for ready money, and 6 pipes of Canary at £15 a pipe from Nicholas Blake 'to pay 1/3 money, the rest at 3 months and 3 months'. He also bought 'sweet' from Thomas Cole, 96 gallons at 4s 6d gallon in April for ready money and a further 60 gallons at the same price in August, to pay at three months.

Pooley's purchases of Rhenish wine had a somewhat ambiguous place in his trade. Rhenish was sometimes assigned to the French and sometimes to the Spanish wine account, presumably because it was used for mixing with French or Spanish wine. It, too, was bought from merchants who seem to have specialised in one type of wine. In May 1656 Michael Buring supplied 2 pipes of Rhenish, one of 142 and the other of 132 gallons, making 274 gallons in all, 'at £7 per alme[31] or 3s 6d per gallon', payable in three months, and in July 1656 John Sheers supplied a ton of Rhenish containing 284 gallons at £5 15s per awm or £40 16s in all, also payable in three months. All Sheers's Rhenish was later 'mixt with Spanish wine'. Finally in March 1657 Gerhard Hacten of London, merchant, supplied '2 fatts of Rhenish wine containing 6 ams 34 gallons at £5 10s per ame'. Pooley was to pay ready money for the total of £37 13s 6d.

Pooley's purchases of wine show that he bought mainly from large London merchants. Barter entered into one or two of these transactions, but the wine was usually bought for ready money or on credit or a mixture of the two. The accounts provide very little

135

evidence on how these payments were actually made. They give the impression that they were usually made in cash, which would be reasonable enough when both buyer and seller were London merchants. There is evidence, however, that payment was sometimes made by bill of exchange. Thus in 1656 Thomas Canham & Co. were paid £110 'by bill drawne per Robert Carter dated 6 December 1656 payable the 6 January 1657, which bill was assigned to John Rebo of Coulchester and the money viz. £110 J. Gray paid to Giles Pooley in Ipswich which G. Pooley paid to Mr. Rebo viz. £100 of it and the other £10 he either hath paid or is to pay to Mr. Canham in full discharge of the sayde £110'. At the same time John Sheers was paid £40 and Robert Hall £19 by bills payable at one month. On 10 April 1657 Nicholas Blake sold to Pooley Canary wine for £90, payable one third in ready money and the rest at three and three months. Blake was paid £30 on 20 June, apparently in cash; he was later paid £30 'by R. C. [Robert Carter] his bill drawne on J.G. [John Gray] the 13 August 1657 at 7 dayes sight to Thomas Norton', and he was paid a further £30 'by bill of exchange drawne per Giles Pooley dated the 4 December 1657 payable 14 dayes after sight per J.G. [John Gray] to Thomas Norton or order for account of dito Blake'. Such payments by bill seem, however, to have been rare.

Pooley's sales of wine are more interesting than his purchases. He sold only a small proportion of his wines in London, and two of these London transactions were barter. The 10 butts of Malaga at £22 a butt supplied to Philip Peddar in 1655 were in truck for cloth, and the 1½ tons of French wine supplied to Edward Turbutt were in barter for Spanish wine. Apart from these cases, less than half a dozen London merchants seem to have bought wine from Pooley, and only three of them bought in any quantity. In 1655 Richard Kerby, wine cooper, and Henry Rowland bought '2 tunn of French wine at £20 per tunn excize free'. They were to pay at one month, which they did. On 6 February 1655 Henry Kem of Westminster bought 4 pipes of Canary for £112 'to pay ready money'. He paid on 17 February when £1 2s was 'spent at receipt of Mr Kem's money' and he was presented with a pair of gloves which cost £1 5s. He sounds a valued customer, but in fact this was his only purchase from Pooley. Indeed Pooley sold his wine mainly in the provinces. In 1655 he sold one pipe of French wine for £10 and one of Spanish for £28 to William Knight of Reading, who was to pay £15 in ready money and the rest in three months. Knight was later allowed £2 0s 10d 'for charges to his cooper, water carriage and cellarige & c.', which suggests that the wine had been shipped up the Thames to Reading. But this was exceptional, for Pooley's main market lay not westward from London but north-eastwards in Suffolk.

Ipswich was the centre of Pooley's provincial trade. There he rented a cellar at £3 per annum and maintained an agent, John Gray, who was paid a commission of 2½ per cent. On January 5 1657 Gray was paid 'for his commission of £882 1s 11d in full of all moneys paide to this day at 2½ per cent £22 1s'. This would seem to represent his payment for the year 1656. Gray's main account was submitted in January of each year; in 1656 this was done in London, but in 1657 it was done at Ipswich when Robert Carter and the bookkeeper who wrote the 'Journall' were present. The bookkeeper spent £3 16s 8d 'in my journey to Suffolke about the wine account' in January 1657, and a further £4 1s 8d was spent 'in our journey amoung the customers'. In the intervals between his main accounts Gray supplied information on his sales of wine; in October 1656 this was done 'by a small noate made up with him at his being in London'. If Gray sometimes came up to London to report, Pooley himself went on occasion to Ipswich as did Edward Lewse, Robert Carter and the bookkeeper. As usual with agents, Gray performed a number of minor services for his employers. In 1655 he was paid 2s for 'carriage of 2 turkeys' and 4s for the carriage of 'a bagg of bookes and a coller of beefe'. Later he supplied Pooley with 8 lb of Spanish tobacco at 7s lb and with firkins of butter at £1 7s a firkin, and paid 6s to Hanna Cowper 'for preserveing cherrys'. Gray seems also to have transmitted 'in Giles Pooley's box from Ipswich' rent which he had received from Anthony Gislingham, Pooley's tenant. On one occasion he was paid 18s by Thomas Pooley for money spent 'in goeing to fetch his rent from Hartest'. The relationship of Thomas to Giles Pooley is uncertain, but in March 1655 Giles paid £8 to 'Mr Peyps for hangings long since sent to Mr Thomas Pooley'. This was presumably the father of the diarist. All these transactions were incidental to Gray's main business which was to sell the wine he received. Most of the wine came from London by sea in Mr. Ford's hoy or John Lambley's hoy or in other named ships. It was usually shipped in the earlier months of the year, from February to

May, except in 1656 when shipments were also made between July and November. Unfortunately there is no evidence on freight charges except for a single entry in July 1655 when £2 16s 2d was paid for 'fraught, wharfidge, portering and warehowse room of 4 tunns of French wine returned from Ipswich'.

Gray sold some wine in Essex where Owin Spann of Harwich bought a pipe of Canary for £30 and a hogshead of French for £5 in 1655; he was 'to pay at 3 monthes'. He bought a further 30 gallons of French in 1656 for £3. Edmond Sommers of Colchester made a single purchase of 4 pipes of Canary at £30 a pipe on 2 November 1655. He was to pay the whole £120 in ready money, which was unusual, and he did in fact pay on 14 December. These sales were exceptional, for most of the wine was sold in Suffolk where the buyers came from a fairly wide range of places. Ipswich itself had both large and small customers. Thus James Betts of Ipswich bought French and Spanish wine for £104 and 30 gallons of Rhenish for £7 10s in 1655, all of which he was to pay at three months. Stephen Green bought a pipe of Canary for £29 in 1655 and a further pipe for £31 the following year, both payable at three months. William Teversham, also of Ipswich, bought 2 pipes of Canary at £30 a pipe in 1655 and a further 3 pipes for £96 in 1657; in between, in 1656, he had only bought 16½ gallons of French wine for £1 19s. With two of his Ipswich customers Gray was unfortunate. George Smith bought a hogshead of French wine for £8 and a pipe of Canary for £30 in 1655. Payment was to be in three months, but £25 was lost by Smith's 'breaking'. John More, who bought a hogshead of French for £6 5s and a pipe of Canary for £31 in 1655 (at three months) also 'broke', and £14 1s was 'lost by his breaking'. At the other end of the scale were the small customers like Mrs Eleanor Methwold of Ipswich who bought 8 gallons of Canary at the low price of 3s 4d gallon, and Robert Clarke who bought 1½ gallons of Spanish wine in 1655 at 6s gallon and a further 2 gallons at 5s in 1656. Presumably such purchases were for direct consumption, and not for re-sale.

Outside Ipswich the chief markets for the wine were Bury St Edmunds, Woodbridge and Snape.[32] At Bury St Edmunds there were two big buyers, Thomas Prettyman and William Bye. Indeed Prettyman was the biggest of all the buyers, provincial or metropolitan. In March 1655 he bought '2 butts new Mallagas' at £28 a butt and '4 pipes new Canaryes' at £30 a pipe. The total of

£176 he was 'to pay £21 7s money, the rest at 3–3 and 3 monthes'.[33] Later in the year he bought another butt of Malaga at £30 which he was to pay in three months. The following year started with a modest purchase in February of one hogshead of claret at £6 and 12 gallons of red wine at 5s gallon, but in June his bill came to £301. It was for 4 pipes Canary and 4 butts Malaga at £32 each, one pipe of Rhenish for £40 and a hogshead of red wine for £5. He was 'to pay [£]30 money, the rest at 3–3 and 3 months viz Michaelmas, Christmas and Lady Day'. In 1657 Prettyman bought only a hogshead of French wine for £7 and a pipe of Canary at £28, payable at three months. William Bye did not operate on Prettyman's scale. He started modestly in January 1655 by buying '1 teerse of French wine containing 40 gallons at 2s 8d per gallon', payable at three months, but later in the year bought a pipe of Canary for £30, a hogshead of French wine for £6 and a hogshead of red wine for £14, again payable at three months. He seems to have made no purchases in 1656, but in 1657 bought 2 pipes of Canary at £34 10s a pipe, this time payable at three months and three months, and 32½ gallons of 'sweet' at 6s gallon, for which he was charged 5s for 'the casque'.

At Woodbridge there were also two big customers, Thomas Raynes and Solomon Smith. Raynes bought French, Spanish and Rhenish wine; he paid £29 for French and £35 for Spanish in 1655, £1 18s 6d for French and £65 10s for Spanish in 1656, and £1 17s for French and £6 15s for Rhenish in 1657. He seems always to have bought for payment in three months. Solomon Smith bought the same three varieties of wine, paying £73 for Spanish in 1655, £51 5s for Spanish and £12 10s for French in 1656 and £4 14s 6d for Rhenish in 1657. He, too, was given three months for payment. At Snape there was only one buyer, Philip Capon. He bought nothing but Canary, 3 pipes of it in 1656 and a hogshead in 1657 at prices ranging from £33 to £36 a pipe, all payable at three months.

Elsewhere in Suffolk Gray sold wine in smaller quantities, though an occasional customer bought by the pipe. Thus Jonathan Betts of 'Budesdale' (presumably Botesdale) and Richard Raynes of Aldeburgh each bought a pipe of Canary for £31 in 1655, Henry Barker of Saxmundham a pipe for £30 in 1656 and John Warren of Wickham Market a pipe for £27 in 1658. Others bought smaller amounts but more often. Thomas Peck of

Stowmarket, for example, bought a hogshead of French wine for £8 and a hogshead of Canary for £19 in 1655 and 2 hogsheads 7 gallons of French for £17 15s in 1656. Similarly Robert Rice of Needham Market bought small quantities of Canary by the gallon on four occasions in 1656 and once in 1657. At Yoxford William Payne was buying Canary by the rundlet and French by the hogshead in November 1656, French and Canary by the hogshead and Malaga by the gallon in December 1656, and Canary by the gallon in April and October 1657. At Debenham David Stiles bought French and Canary wine by the gallon in 1656 and 1658. Finally some customers made a single purchase of less than a pipe; Lionel Allum of Claydon 8 gallons of Canary in 1655, Ralph Ingram of Thwaite 17½ gallons of French in 1656, Richard Rashbrooke of Woolpit a hogshead of Canary in 1657, and James Gilson of Sudbury a hogshead of Canary in 1658.

All these customers, great and small, bought their wine very largely on credit, paying for it in three months or in instalments at three-monthly intervals. It is doubtful whether they always kept rigidly to their times of payment. Thus in 1655 Prettyman should have paid his bill of £206 in March, June, September and December of that year, but in fact he paid £21 7s in April, £40 sometime between April and August, £10 in August, £50 in October, £28 in November 1655 and £56 13s in January 1656. Similarly Philip Capon should have paid £33 for a pipe of Canary by June 1656, but he seems to have paid in instalments, the last of them in December 1656. The customers, again both large and small, seem to have paid John Gray in cash and not by inland bills. They did not apparently remit money direct to Pooley in London. Gray in turn appears to have sent some of the proceeds of his sales to London in the form of cash or paid them to Pooley in Ipswich. Some were remitted by bill, as in 1655 when Pooley received £75 from Gray, 'which J. Gray did Exchange[34] up to London', or again in March 1656 when he received £257 9s by a 'bill drawne per Richard Greene of Colchester', which probably represents such a remittance, or in 1657 when Carter drew a bill on Gray payable to Thomas Norton.[35] There are, however, few clear references to remittance by bill. Perhaps the nearness of Ipswich to London and the visits of Gray to London and of Pooley, Carter and Lewse to Ipswich made such remittances less necessary.

It is not easy to see what pattern, if any, this provincial trade conformed to. Geographically the centre was Ipswich, and the lines of trade radiated from there. North-westwards the line seems to have run through Claydon, Needham Market, Stowmarket and Woolpit to Bury St Edmunds. North-eastwards the line ran from Ipswich through Woodbridge, Wickham Market and Saxmundham to Yoxford, with a branch to Snape and Aldeburgh. Northwards the links may have been Ipswich to Debenham, Thwaite and Botesdale. There was no extension into Norfolk except on one occasion when wine was sent to George Miris of Norwich, but was in fact sold to Henry Pendleton, who may have been a Norwich man. Wine for Norfolk was more likely to be distributed from King's Lynn and from the Great Yarmouth–Norwich axis. Commercially the centre of Pooley's provincial trade was also Ipswich, but only a minority of the customers lived there. Those who did live in the town seem to have bought their wine for different purposes. The very small purchasers must presumably have been buying for their own consumption, which implies that Gray was selling a little of his wine by retail. This category would include Major Harvey who bought 9 gallons of Canary at 5s gallon in 1656 and a further 2 gallons at the same price in 1658, and Robert Rednall, probably the haberdasher of that name,[36] who bought 11 gallons 2 pints of French wine at 2s 4d gallon and 6 gallons 6 pints of Spanish wine at 6s gallon in 1657. It is not clear how far up the scale this retail buying went, but men like James Betts, William Teversham and Stephen Green were almost certainly buying for re-sale. Green, for example, was the landlord of the Greyhound Inn in Ipswich.[37] It is likely that this pattern was repeated in the other Suffolk towns and there too the small sales were retail and the larger sales were wholesale. If that is true, then most of the wine was sold wholesale, presumably to wine merchants or innkeepers. This would be a normal form of trade for a London merchant to pursue in the provinces. Indeed it is rather surprising that Gray engaged in so many petty transactions, apparently of a retail nature.

Gray was an agent working on commission and as such was in charge of the trade based on Ipswich. He had nothing to do with the purchase or sale of wine in London. As most of the wine was bought in London and sold in Suffolk, Gray was responsible for most of the selling. His accounts, in so far as they are incorporated in the 'Journall', are not in a form which allows the profit and loss of the Suffolk trade to be determined. The accounts in the journal deal with the whole of the wine trade. They are meagre for 1654 when the trade was small, and no conclusions on profits can be drawn for that year. For 1655 and 1656 the position is clearer. During those two years the wine trade was conducted by a partnership of Giles Pooley and Robert Carter, with whom Pooley lodged. Carter put some capital into the partnership, apparently £150, for which he received interest at 6 per cent. His fairly frequent journeys to Ipswich show that he was an active partner. The two partners made up their accounts in January 1657 showing the 'Proffitt and losse gayned by God's blessing by this wine trade since January 1654 [1654/5] now 2 years'. The profit on Spanish wine was £287 7s 10d and on French wine £44 12s 3d, making a total of £332. As Pooley was 'to have ¾ of the proffitt and R.C. ¼', Pooley's 'divident' was £249 and Carter's £83. It is interesting to compare this profit with the figures for purchases and sales during the two years. In 1655 the purchases were: Spanish wine £984 and French wine £178;[38] the sales were Spanish £1,268 and French £257. The figures for 1656 were: purchases of Spanish £488[39] and of French £200;[40] sales of Spanish £815 and of French £185.[41] Thus over the two years purchases were £1,805 and sales £2,527. The difference was £722 of which £332 was profit (or about 13 per cent on the sales) and £390 presumably expenses. But too much should not be made of such figures, for they are complicated by the barter transactions, the payment of excise and the lack of knowledge about stock carried over. Even so, the trade was obviously profitable in 1655 and 1656, for Pooley's profit of £249 was not to be sneezed at in the mid seventeenth century. For 1657 there is no profit and loss account, though there is some evidence that the partnership continued. By then the trade had greatly declined: purchases of Spanish wine amounted to only £265[42] and of French to £2 10s, while sales were Spanish £395 and French £20. The trade certainly continued into 1658, when Gray was still in charge at Ipswich, but the accounts end in March of that year.

Even for the years when the accounts are very full, it is difficult to work out any exact relationship between buying and selling prices or to explain some of the variations in prices. Thus in 1655 Canary was bought at prices ranging from £12 to £36 a pipe, and sold at prices ranging from £30 to £35 a pipe; Malaga cost from

£15 to £31 a pipe (assuming a butt was equal to a pipe) and sold at from £21 to £30. In 1656 Canary was bought at £26 a pipe and sold at £32 to £38 a pipe; Malaga cost £21 to £24 a pipe and sold at £27 to £32. There is much less information on the prices of French wine, which was a great deal cheaper than Spanish. In 1655 French wine was bought at £11 and £22 ton (or £5 10s and £11 a pipe) and sold at £16 to £32 ton (or £8 to £16 a pipe); in 1656 it seems to have cost £24 ton and been sold at £20 to £36 ton. Finally the Rhenish wine was bought and sold by a variety of measures, of which the basic ones were the gallon and the awm or aam of 40 gallons. In 1655 30 gallons of Rhenish were bought at 4s 6d and sold at 5s gallon. The following year a ton of 284 gallons was bought for £40 16s, which was calculated at £5 15s per awm, and a pipe of Rhenish was sold for £40, which was so high a price that it may have been a mistake for a ton. In fact not much Rhenish was sold separately, for it was bought to mix with other wines, a practice which complicates the question of prices. It even complicated Pooley's accounts; a ton of Rhenish bought in 1656 for £40 16s was bought on the French wine account, but as the Rhenish was actually 'mixt with Spanish wine', Spanish wine had to be made debtor to French wine for £40 16s. Similarly 30 gallons of 'sweete' were bought in 1657 'to put in the French wines at Ipswich'. The 'sweete' itself might be treated or perhaps even manufactured; in 1657 4 cwt of 'sugger' was bought for £17 10s 'to make sweete' and was made into '1 hogshead 32 gallons sweete'. The costs included £2 7s 3d for 'a brass pan, iron furnace &c.' and £1 0s 1d 'charges of makeing 4 cwt sugger into 1 hogshead ½ of sweete'. Whatever may be the ethics of all this, such practices can hardly help the historians of prices.

These variations in the price of wine may have been caused by a great many factors. They were too great to result from mere differences in the conditions of purchase and sale in the sense that wine might be bought and sold for ready money or future payment. Indeed much of the wine was bought and sold for future payment, usually in three months. Differences in quality are a more likely cause of variations in price, but the accounts reveal nothing of this unless the single reference in 1655 to 'new Mallagas' and 'new Canaryes' indicated superior quality, on the assumption that seventeenth-century wine deteriorated rather than improved with age. But there was nothing in the price of these new wines to suggest superior (or inferior) quality. Differences in measures are a possible cause of price variation, for it is not known whether the ton or pipe or butt or hogshead was always of uniform size. Nor, of course, is it known whether it was always full. In December 1656 Robert Dix bought 3 hogsheads of French wine 'wanting 8 inches of full one of them' and was later allowed 11s for the short measure. The wine casks were subject to 'leakige' which was recorded in the accounts. In 1655, of the wine sent to Ipswich French wine 'lost per leakige 1 hogshead and 30 gallons' and Spanish wine 1 pipe, 1 hogshead and $50\frac{3}{4}$ gallons. The following year the losses by leakage were heavier, amounting to 1 pipe and 60 gallons of Canary and 1 hogshead and $17\frac{1}{4}$ gallons of French in London, and 1 pipe $24\frac{1}{2}$ gallons of Canary and 1 hogshead $18\frac{1}{2}$ gallons of French in Ipswich. Such losses were no doubt recorded because it was possible to claim a rebate of excise duty for them.

Excise duty was another, and perhaps the most important, factor in complicating the interpretation of wine prices. Under an Ordinance of 17 March 1654 an excise duty of £6 was to be levied on every ton of wine, and a ton was said to be equivalent to 2 butts or 2 pipes or 4 hogsheads. The duty was 'to bee paid by the first buyer'.[43] As Pooley does not seem to have imported his wine, it is probable that he was usually the 'first buyer', and therefore had to pay the excise. Thus on 14 May 1655 he bought 8 butts of Malaga from Samuel Willson, merchant of London, for £19 a butt and on 22 June paid £7 15s for the excise on three of these butts. Again, on 2 March 1655 2 pipes of Canary were sent to John Gray 'for which paid excize', and the excise of £5 was paid the same day. Wine was sent to Gray with the statement 'excize taken of from accompt here' or 'excize free', which apparently meant that Pooley had paid the excise in London. This was not always done, however, for in some cases Gray paid the excise in Ipswich. In 1655 he paid the Commissioners of Excize £21 'for excize of Spanish wine' he had sold, and in 1656 he paid Major Moll and Captain Stebing £24 15s for excise of wines sent to Ipswich. The accounts suggest that Pooley, or Gray as his agent, paid the excise on the wine he bought, which would mean that the excise duty was not included in the buying price but was included in the price of the wine he sold. It is not certain that this was true in all cases. On 4 April 1655, Pooley bought a pipe of Canary for £25 from Robert

Hall of London, wine cooper, with a note that 'it was first bought for £26 and he pay the excize, afterward it was agreed for £25 and wee pay the excize'. Later purchases from Hall at £26 a pipe might imply that he was then paying the excise. The difference of £1 was less than the excise payable on a pipe of Canary, which should have been £3 (at £6 ton), but in all cases except one where the excise was recorded it was less than £6 ton. Thus in 1655 £5 was paid on a ton of Canary and £5 3s 4d on a ton of Malaga; on French wine the payment was £4 5s in one case and £5 in another. The reason for this underpayment is not clear, for little work seems to have been done on the excise in this period. The only relevant point is perhaps the obvious one, namely that the existence of an excise duty affects the relationship between buying and selling prices and makes it more difficult to calculate the real difference between the two.

Pooley's activities as a London merchant engaged in the inland trade raise many questions which cannot be answered from the surviving accounts. It is not known, for example, why his cloth trade declined after 1655 or why his wine trade declined also after 1655. It could be argued that the cloth trade became unprofitable, but the reasons for this are unclear. It could also be argued that the wine trade, which depended heavily on Spanish wine, declined because the import of that wine became difficult after Cromwell's breach with Spain, but again this would be difficult to prove. Even if such questions cannot be answered satisfactorily from the accounts, the latter do provide sufficient material for a case study. Whether it was a typical case is very doubtful. The combination of the cloth trade and the wine trade seems unusual. The two trades were linked to a slight extent in London by the barter of cloth for wine and of wine for cloth, but in the provinces it is difficult to find any connection between the purchase of cloth in Norfolk and the sale of wine in Suffolk. If Pooley had dealt in Suffolk cloth the combination might have appeared more logical. Instead he traded in two areas and in two commodities which involved him in a one-way traffic in goods with each area; there is no evidence that he brought any goods from Suffolk or, except in one instance, that he sent any goods to Norfolk. One-way traffic in goods was not unusual, as the Rodes partnership shows, but it may have been more unusual to engage in two branches of it. Moreover Pooley's trade was no simple exchange between London and the provinces; he bought more cloth in London than in

Norfolk and sold wine in London as well as in Suffolk. Again it would be interesting to know how typical this was, for it created additional middlemen in the London trade, where Pooley bought cloth or wine from one merchant only to sell it to another. These purely metropolitan transactions are less interesting than the provincial ones, which provide some evidence on how London received goods from and supplied goods to the provinces. That circulation of goods was important not only to London but to the provincial economy as well.

Notes

1. The letters are in the House of Lords Record Office. They are mentioned in *H.M.C. Third Report*, p. 11.
2. Perhaps a journeyman or apprentice. He was once referred to as Anne Gray's 'man'.
3. Probably a journeyman assistant.
4. The accounts are in the Cavendish of Holker MSS. (DD Ca/1/46) in L.R.O. They came to the Cavendishes through marriage with the Lowther family, one of whom, Alderman Robert Lowther, was a London merchant who seems to have had some business connection with Giles Pooley.
5. On the withdrawal of English merchants from the Canaries in 1655 see R. Davies, ed., *The life of Marmaduke Rawdon of York*, Camden Soc., lxxxv (1863), 39–67.
6. Presumably Faro in Portugal.
7. It is possible that this trade in indigo was done in partnership with Holcroft.
8. On the Norfolk cloth industry see K. J. Allison, 'The Norfolk worsted industry in the sixteenth and seventeenth centuries', *Yorkshire Bulletin of Economic and Social Research*, 12 (1960), pp. 73–83, 13 (1961), pp. 61–77.
9. There is some evidence that Pooley had been engaged in the Norwich cloth trade as early as 1640 when he was in partnership with Samuel Chapman and Francis Cooke (Cavendish of Holker MSS., DD Ca/1/105 (L.R.O.).
10. One of the white hair russells was given as $26\frac{3}{4}$ yds and two were 24 yds each.
11. This has not been identified; it is not in *O.E.D.*
12. Perhaps a variant of duretto which *O.E.D.* defines as 'a coarse

146

stout stuff". They were sometimes described as silk and sometimes as worsted.

[13] Italiano (in *O.E.D.* under 'satinisco'); they cost £4 each.

[14] It was 23½ yds long and cost 5s 6d yd.

[15] Not identified; it is not in *O.E.D.*

[16] Cheyneys, a Norwich stuff, probably worsted.

[17] Not identified; it is not in *O.E.D.*

[18] Fabric with a chequered pattern.

[19] Perhaps a variant of stamin or tammy.

[20] Probably a colour, pink or crimson; 'in grain' means dyed with kermes.

[21] *O.E.D.* gives a strong stuff originally of silk, afterwards worsted, and dates it from 1656.

[22] Satinisco, an inferior quality of satin.

[23] *O.E.D.* gives it as a modern (1787) revival of barracan, a coarse camlet.

[24] Perhaps the Richard Young who was importing sugar from Barbados in 1658 (P. McGrath, ed., *Merchants and merchandise in seventeenth-century Bristol*, Bristol Record Soc., xix (1955), 250 n.

[25] He paid £30 in April and £52 12s in June 1655.

[26] Norwich stuffs were exported from Bristol in the 1670s (McGrath, *op. cit.*, pp. 265–6, 268, 273).

[27] An interesting example of the cost of broadcloth as compared with the new draperies.

[28] Meaning that half was to be paid in four months and the other half in eight months.

[29] This entry is quite clear, but the price is so low as to suggest that ton is a mistake for pipe or butt (i.e. half a ton).

[30] C. H. Firth and R. S. Rait, *Acts and Ordinances of the Interregnum*, ii. 239–40, 1129.

[31] The awm was a measure usually of 40 gallons.

[32] For the country trade of a sixteenth-century Ipswich merchant see J. Webb, *Great Tooley of Ipswich*, ch. v.

[33] That is at three, six and nine months.

[34] The word is contracted in the MS., but this is what it seems to mean.

[35] *Supra*, p. 136.

[36] Williamson, iii. 1087.

[37] *Ibid.*, iii. 1086.

[38] Including £6 15s for Rhenish.
[39] Including £4 17s for Rhenish.
[40] Including £88 for Rhenish.
[41] Including £40 for Rhenish.
[42] Including £37 for Rhenish.
[43] C. H. Firth and R. S. Rait, *Acts and Ordinances of the Interregnum*, ii. 848.

INDEX

154